THE BEST INVESTMENT

THE BEST
INVESTMENT
Land in a Loving Community

BY DAVID W. FELDER

WELLINGTON PRESS

The Best Investment: Land In A Loving Community

Wellington Press Edition; March 1983
Copyright © 1982 by David W. Felder

ISBN 0-910959-00-5
Library of Congress Catalog Card Number 86-61882

Cover painting by Janet Falciglia
Design and Photography by Glenn Sharron
Typography by RapidoGraphics of Tallahassee
Printed in the U.S. by Rose Printing Co.

The name of the community described in this book and many of the facts
have been changed to protect the privacy of community members. The
author and publisher make no claim to literal accuracy.

Copies of this book may be obtained by sending $10 to the publisher, which
covers postage, handling, and any sales tax that may apply.

Wellington Press
P.O. Box 13504
Tallahassee, FL 32308

Wellington Press is a Division of Co-operative Enterprises, Inc.

To my parents,
Jack and Evelyn Felder;
and to Judy.

C̲T̲A̲B̲L̲E̲ O̲F̲ S̲
ONTENTS

I. THE SIMPLE LIFESTYLE ALTERNATIVE

2 **Chapter One**
YOUR CHOICE: MAKE MORE OR CONSUME LESS
Why We Have to Live on Less ◆ Ways of Coping ◆ Is the Simple Lifestyle for You ◆ My Own Case

8 **Chapter Two**
GOING IT ALONE OR WITH OTHERS
My View of the Simple Lifestyle ◆ The Individual Route ◆ The Community Route ◆ Advantages of the Community Route

14 **Chapter Three**
LIVING BETTER ON LESS
Living Comfortably on Ten Thousand a Year ◆ Actual Budgets ◆ Ways of Saving ◆ Homes ◆ Entertainment ◆ Tools ◆ Heating

II. WAYS OF SAVING

28 **Chapter Four**
SAVING ON HOME CONSTRUCTION
Paying for Your Land ◆ Building a Shed ◆ Electrical Service ◆ Know Your Land Before You Build ◆ Four Ways to Get a House ◆ Move a House ◆ Be the Contractor ◆ Build with a Buddy ◆ Do Part or All Yourself ◆ Post and Beam Construction ◆ Domes ◆ Ways of Getting Building Materials ◆ Demolition

44 **Chapter Five**
PRODUCING YOUR OWN FOOD
The Joys of Gardening ◆ Chickens ◆ Goats

54 **Chapter Six**
BARTERING IN THE COMMUNITY
How Barter Works ◆ A Barter Economy

58 Chapter Seven
    INVESTING FOR PEOPLE
    WHO WANT TO RETIRE YOUNG
    Planning Your Finances ◆ Your First Investments ◆ The
    Traditional Investments

III. COMMUNITY DYNAMICS

66 Chapter Eight
    STARTING A COMMUNITY
    It Begins with Meetings ◆ Deciding What Type of
    Community You Want ◆ Land Co-operatives ◆
    Mistakes to Avoid

74 Chapter Nine
    COMMUNITY DECISION MAKING
    Majority Rule ◆ Consensual Decision Making ◆
    Professional Planning

82 Chapter Ten
    GETTING THINGS DONE
    Pitfalls to Avoid ◆ How to Run Meetings ◆ The
    Standard Code of Co-operative Procedure ◆ Getting
    People to Work ◆ Prisoners of Our Own Dogma

90 Chapter Eleven
    BUILDING A SENSE OF COMMUNITY
    Spiritual Benefits of a Community ◆ Respect for
    Community Property ◆ Community Celebrations ◆
    Thanksgiving ◆ Christmas ◆ Easter and Passover ◆ A
    Holiday of Our Own ◆ Marriages on the Land ◆ Parties

IV. MOVING TO YOUR LAND

100 Chapter Twelve
    BUYING YOUR LAND
    Getting Ready ◆ Selecting Land ◆ Figuring the Sales
    Price ◆ Your Down Payment ◆ Community Loan
    Program ◆ Project Financial Summary ◆ Co-signers for
    the Bank Loan ◆ Cash Flow Projections ◆ Building Your
    Net Worth ◆ Getting Deeds ◆ Mistakes and Surprises

110   Chapter Thirteen
PREPARING FOR CONSTRUCTION
Surveying the Land ◆ Planning the Land ◆ Dividing
the Land ◆ Roads ◆ Electricity ◆ Water

118   Chapter Fourteen
COMMUNITY PROJECTS
Providing Activities for Children ◆ Fighting Fires ◆
Controlling Politicians ◆ Controlling Mosquitoes

V. WHAT YOU CAN ACHIEVE

130   Chapter Fifteen
LIVING YOUR DREAMS
Financial Independence Is a Community Affair ◆
Community Based Businesses ◆ Agriculture ◆ A
Nonprofit Research Institute ◆ Some Personal Dreams

144   Chapter Sixteen
IT'S MORE THAN AN INVESTMENT
Making the World Better ◆ Utopian Communities: Past
and Present ◆ Providing an Alternative ◆ Helping to
Preserve Scarce Resources ◆ Being a Center for Change

APPENDIX

154   Appendix One
MODEL SET OF COVENANTS
AND RESTRICTIONS

162   Appendix Two
LAND CO-OP CONSULTANTS

PREFACE

The best investment I ever made was to buy land in a loving community of about one hundred people. Because of the nature of the community, people helped each other to build homes. I, along with others, ended up owning a home with no mortgage. My investment in land made it possible for me first to apply payments that had been going for rent to the purchase of materials for my house, and second to apply these same funds to investments once my house was completed. An investment that allows you to redirect money you are spending on rent or mortgage toward assuring you the security of owning a home outright and having an investment income is the best investment you can make. When you read about the community I describe, you will learn that buying land in a loving community is more than a superb investment. As great as the material benefits are, the spiritual benefits are even greater.

The Simple Lifestyle Alternative

PART ONE

CHAPTER
• ONE •

YOUR CHOICE:
MAKE MORE OR CONSUME LESS

There are two ways of keeping up with inflation. You can make more or you can learn to live on less. It is of course desirable to do both. But for many people there is no way to increase income substantially; it therefore becomes imperative for many individuals that they learn to live on less.

Why We Have to Live on Less

It is also imperative that we as a nation learn to live on less. The United States, with five percent of the world's people, cannot continue to consume thirty percent of the world's goods. Our domination of other countries is coming to an end. Other nations whose resources we depend upon are insisting on a greater share of the world's wealth. Even if a redistribution of the world's wealth were not necessary, there are other factors that prevent our increasing our consumption.

First, there is our depletion of nonrenewable resources such as oil. No supply side economics can create an endless supply of resources that are limited on our planet. The shortage of oil will soon be followed by a shortage of certain metals, such as silver and copper. As population increases, and as underdeveloped countries try to develop, the demand for almost everything will increase. Prices on scarce items will rise, and our ability to consume will fall.

Second, there is a frightening loss of precious topsoil occurring worldwide. One inch of topsoil takes from one to three hundred years to develop. We are destroying our precious soil by asphalting it over and destroying it with chemicals. Much of the world's farming is now done with petrochemicals that burn the topsoil. Once oil runs out, we will have to grow our food on impoverished lands. Already the reduction of farm lands has caused food prices to rise.

Third, someday soon we will have to clean up the mess we have made of our environment. Six hundred million tons of pollutants are released every year. Some areas, such as the land by the Love Canal, are already uninhabitable. It has been estimated that there are one hundred potential "Love Canal sites" throughout the country right now. It is going to be very expensive to get rid of the poisons we have been releasing. When we start paying these costs, our consumption will have to be reduced.

As if the problems due to the growth of population and the increase in development were not enough, we face problems due to the idiocy of some of the world's politicians. The insane policies guided by the strategy of Mutual Assured Destruction (MAD) continue. The amount of money spent on armaments continues to increase at a point in history when we cannot afford an arms race. The money for the arms race will of course have to come either out of money individuals have to spend or the buying power of their money.

Our nation, and indeed the world, cannot sustain continued unlimited growth. Some growth may be possible, but some limits on our rate of growth are inevitable. Particular individuals may be able to buck the tide, but as a nation we are going to have to learn to live on less.

The idea that the answer to our national problems is economic growth, and to our personal problems is increasing our incomes, is increasingly being exposed as false. Economists are starting to question the relationship between GNP figures and human welfare. That expenditures due to automobile accidents and increases in interest rates raise the GNP shows that the amount spent does not have much to do with welfare. Individuals are also beginning to realize that they have to do more than increase their incomes in order to improve their lives. The futility of the bind that most people are in is illuminated by examining the plight of a typical American family, the Smiths.

Ways of Coping

Joe and Mary Smith rent an apartment in one of the better sections of a large city. They moved up to living where they are now from less expensive apartments and can't really afford the rent they pay. But they feel that it is important to live in a good section for the sake of the children and security. Joe and Mary wish they could afford to send their children to a private school, but the cost is prohibitive. As it is, with both of them working they are barely able to get by. They live in constant fear of losing their jobs and being

4

forced to move into a less desirable neighborhood. Their dream is that someday they will be able to move by raising the down payment for a home of their own in the suburbs.

Compare the situation of Joe and Mary Smith with that of Harold and Susan Barkley. Harold and Susan got together with other people to form their own community. Instead of paying more and more to move into better and better neighborhoods, these people started from scratch and created a community of their own, a real community where people know each other. Instead of paying $10,000 for a down payment and owing $60,000 at fourteen percent, Harold and Susan paid $1,000 down for an acre of land and built a home. After spending $5,000, they had an unfinished house they could live in and were able to use the money that had been going for rent to finish their house. Within five years they owned a finished house and land outright with no mortgage whatsoever. They enjoy their loving community, the children go to the community's school, and Harold and Susan are now able to live on much less thanks to heating with wood, growing vegetables, and having a house with no mortgage.

Is the Simple Lifestyle for You?

Is the simple lifestyle alternative really possible for most people? I believe it is. It is not without sacrifices. Not everyone is willing to live in an unfinished house. But for those who don't mind some hardships, the simple lifestyle I describe in this book is a real alternative. In what follows I'll show you how to live better on less. If you follow my advice, you'll end up owning a house with no mortgage in a loving community.

My Own Case

In my own case, I was able to pay off my land and house while earning a teacher's salary of $12,000. I decided to simplify my life after experiencing a year of unemployment. At that time I had to struggle with a home mortgage. I then decided that I would set myself up so that if I was ever without a job again, I would be able to enjoy myself. And indeed, now I can relax several months every summer because I am able to live well within my means.

I have neighbors who are able to travel for months on end, secure in the knowledge that it costs them nothing to maintain their homes. People are now able to live comfortably on under $10,000 a year. These are people who own their own homes, work at home, and have time to be with their children.

Is the simple lifestyle alternative for you? This book is designed to help you decide. I organized it so you can see your options. The next chapter poses the question of whether you should try to do it alone or with a community. Another chapter outlines the options you have in building a home. In another chapter I tell you just enough about growing vegetables and raising livestock so you can decide if that is for you. While the alternative I discuss may not be for everyone, the simple lifestyle is desirable for most people, and you will do yourself a service in examining it.

CHAPTER
· TWO ·

GOING IT ALONE OR
WITH OTHERS

Most books on living a simpler lifestyle center on how individuals can go off by themselves. Going off into the middle of nowhere by yourself, to do everything by yourself, is not my idea of living a good life. I don't feel any need to prove that I can live without other people. Maybe I could, maybe I couldn't, but it wouldn't be much of an existence. My idea of a simple lifestyle involves living a self-determined life surrounded by warm friends and neighbors. I actually live in a community of about a hundred people who have formed an intentional community. People here live with all the advantages of civilization and few of the hassles. We are able to live better on less.

My View of the Simple Lifestyle

Living simply, by my definition, means maximizing the advantages of modern society and minimizing the disadvantages. This means having a car but not having to commute daily to an unsatisfactory job. Having a choice between buying organic food or growing your own, but avoiding foods with carcinogens, is another aspect of the simple life. It means that you live a life you design. You can plan your day according to your needs and desires.

The Individual Route

There are many books on simplifying your life that present a rustic individual route. These books appeal to individuals who want to go out into the woods by themselves and prove that they can survive without other people. In their book *Living the Good Life*, Scott and Helen Nearing show that it is possible for two individuals to clear land without the aid of tractors and that people can live without electricity. I don't doubt that people can do such things but wonder why they should want to. I enjoy the company of my neighbors and feel no need to prove that I can do without them. I enjoy the benefits of electricity and don't feel any need to do without this modern convenience. A good and simple life can still contain the advantages of civilization, such as human community and technological innovations.

The Community Route

This book, then, is about the community route to the simple lifestyle alternative. Most books on alternate lifestyles detail how one family can attempt to be self-sufficient. I believe, though, that the community route is much more desirable, as I will try to convince you in the following pages. Throughout the book, by using the particular achievements of my own community, I will be showing what can be accomplished with the community route.

I joined the community of which I am a member, the Misty Hills Land Co-operative (M.L.C.), because of a speech at an organizational meeting. The organizer of the co-op contrasted the idea of buying one acre on your own with the idea of buying an acre in an intentional community:

> If you buy land on your own, you have the fear that someone will build something ugly next to you. With such a fear you have to try to buy buffer land around your home. But the extra acres you pay for are simply that: a buffer. Unless you're a serious farmer, you're not going to farm twenty acres, and you won't even walk on all twenty. Buying twenty acres merely for protection is a waste of your resources. You would do better to buy one acre in a protected community.

Protecting your land and quality of life can be done better when you buy land with others. When you buy land with a group of people who respect nature, your neighbor's land serves as a buffer for you. You know that the acres around you will always be natural because the community has restrictions on the removal of trees. You can still walk in the woods because there are easements guaranteeing your right to walk.

I can say, with pleasure, that all the advantages the organizer promised were real. But they are not the only ones. After the co-op was set up, many nice things started to happen that I did not foresee. With hindsight I realize now that tremendous energy is created when

10

a group of people form a community together. And energy creates advantages, both spiritual and economic.

Some advantages exist no matter how small the community; other advantages depend upon size. I will be reporting specifically on my own community, which consists of slightly more than one hundred households, but you will be able to see which benefits are applicable to your group. For convenience I will use the figure of one hundred families at the M.L.C., which allows us to think in terms of percentages. Remember, though, there is nothing magic about this number; a community of eight persons would enjoy many of the same advantages.

Advantages of the Community Route

When you get many households together to form an alternate community, a tremendous amount of purchasing power is created. Suddenly there is enough construction going on to support members of the community as carpenters and to form a good sized construction company. The financial arrangements for the co-op can employ someone as a bookkeeper; the job of running the development can employ someone as a coordinator. Childcare for a community of one hundred families can provide someone with work. With ingenuity dozens of jobs can be created. One woman in our co-op supports herself by making lunches for many of the people who still work outside the co-operative. It is reasonable to expect that as soon as a hundred families get together in an alternate community, jobs will be created for twenty-five people—people who will be on their way to an independent, simple lifestyle.

More than a quarter of the inhabitants of the M.L.C. have been able to drop out of nine-to-five jobs. All the co-op members are getting out from under making payments on their homes. More than half live in homes that have no mortgages. These economic benefits are overwhelming, but even more important are the spiritual benefits of living in a loving community.

I have had some of the greatest highs of my life from being with my neighbors at our community gatherings. Seeing beautiful children playing together in our community center or having a Thanksgiving meal with a hundred others in the community gives me a wonderful feeling. The emotional ties that we have forged are something that cannot be measured. The community route to a simpler lifestyle, forming a community with others, can give you spiritual benefits you cannot obtain by yourself.

Many of the books on how to do it alone are based on the premise that you can only be self-sufficient if you do everything for yourself. So these books describe how one family can do everything for themselves. But they forget why people want to be self-sufficient in the first place. People want to have things set up so that their lives are not dependent on the economic cycle of boom and bust, and more recently, so their lives will not be threatened if the oil supply is shut off. Doing everything for oneself is one way of insuring that all the necessities of life are at hand. The community route is another way of achieving the exact same goal.

With the community route all the necessities of life are in the community rather than in each household. People are able to specialize and to trade the things they produce. Through the use of barter people can insulate themselves from the uncertainties of the larger economy.

CHAPTER
• THREE •

LIVING BETTER ON LESS

Many families on the land co-op live comfortably on under $10,000 a year. Others will be able to live well on that amount once they get their homes completed. In order to reach the happy point of having a home and land paid for, some people live in cramped quarters with a transitional budget. They do this to hasten the day when they will be able to have the sort of budget those who have completed homes enjoy. I will provide some examples of both transitional budgets and the budgets of settled people.

Living Comfortably on Ten Thousand a Year

I present here the budgets of actual people in my community but will disguise some facts about the people to protect their privacy. The budgets are divided into fixed expenses and variable expenses.

Fixed expenses	Variable expenses
Rent/Mortgage/Loans	Clothing
Food	Cleaning
Utilities	Medical/Drugs
electricity	Books/Periodicals
gas	Recreation
firewood	movies
Transportation	eating out
Insurance	vacations
	Contributions
	Home Improvement
	Child Care

I'll start with the budgets of single individuals, then look at couples who have no children, and finally examine the budget of a family with three children.

Ray Stanley's Budget

Ray's house is paid for. He built his 576 square foot house mostly from materials he obtained from tearing down condemned houses. Ray grows most of his food, so his monthly food bill is only $15. He heats with firewood he cuts himself, so his total utility bill is only $7.50 a month for lights and refrigerator, plus $1.65 a month for a gas stove. Ray has a solar water heater which helps account for the phenomenally low electric bill. Ray's biggest expense is a $100 a month payment on a car, which will end within a year. His next biggest expense is buying gas for the car, which comes to $80 a month. All of his fixed payments together, including insurance, phone, car, house, etc., come to $235 a month or under $3,000 a year. Once the car is paid for, Ray's total fixed expenses will be under $2,000 a year.

Ray actually spends more than the minimum necessary to live because he spends an average of $20 a month on clothes and about $77 a month on eating out and entertainment. He also makes contributions to causes and subscribes to several magazines. His total variable expenses come to $124 a month or $1,488 a year. Ray estimates that he spends between $4,000 and $5,000 a year.

What is it like to live on under $5,000 a year? Ray is eating healthy food and living in his own home. Every year at Christmas time he takes a trip south to the Florida Keys. Within the past few years he has made trips across the country. Ray earns his living as a carpenter and usually finds work within our community. He supplements this by selling vegetables to neighbors. When I asked if he had achieved his goals in regard to self-sufficiency, Ray replied that his goals have expanded with time. A year ago Ray had neither phone nor car. That year he had only a motorcycle. The year before he had no motor vehicle. That means that Ray used to live on less than $3,000 a year because his car payments and gas for the car cost $2,000 of his $5,000 a year budget. Unlike others who are living more and more simply, Ray has been spending more each year.

Rosa Hunt's Budget

Rosa Hunt is not into construction. She had a community based construction company build a 900 square foot frame house for her for under $17,000. Her house has central heat and air, a dishwasher, and all the modern conveniences. Rosa doesn't use the air conditioning any more than she has to, which allows her to keep her utilities down to $25 a month. Her only monthly expenses, other than the $135 mortgage payment on her house, are $40 for gas for her car, $50 for insurance, and $75 for food. Her total fixed expenses are $334 a month or about $4,000 a year.

Rosa doesn't spend much on variable expenses. She spends practically nothing on clothes because she makes them herself, and she spends only $2.50 a month for cleaning. Her average monthly expense for eating out and entertainment is $70. This means that Rosa Hunt lives on under $5,000 a year. Rosa earns more than she needs by producing hand-painted T shirts in her home using an air brush. She is a true artist, and her shirts are highly prized. For three years she has been self-employed, and her business is going strong. With expenses under $5,000 a year, Rosa Hunt is able to save.

George and Debbie Hycliff

The Hycliffs have a new car and are building a 1,900 square foot house. The main expense of the Hycliff family is building materials for their home. Before moving into the land co-op, their main expense was rent. As soon as they moved out, they were able to use the money that had been going for rent for building their own home. The Hycliffs do not live cheaply at present, but once their home and car are paid for, their expenses will drop considerably.

The fixed expenses of the Hycliffs include $200 a month for transportation, which includes payments on a new car and gas for their car and truck. They have a couple of loans that total $400 a month that will be paid up within a year. Their average electric bill for their 1,900 square foot house is only $30 because they have a gas stove and gas hot water heater. All their fixed expenses, including property taxes and food at $200 a month, total $909 a month or about $11,000 a year. A year from now, when the car is paid for and the other loans are paid up, the fixed expenses should drop to $400 a month or about $5,000 a year.

The Hycliffs' main expense is their house. They have set the goal of having their home completed and paid for within two years and are reaching that goal. Under variable expenses they list $500 a month for materials to finish their house. I include this figure as a variable expense because the exact amount they spend each month is up to them, while the loans they took out mostly for building materials must be paid each month. All totalled, the Hycliffs are spending almost $1,000 a month for their home. This is not excessive when one considers that their 1,900 square foot house would cost $76,000 for a contractor to build. In two years the Hycliffs will own their $76,000 home with no mortgages.

George and Debbie Hycliff live very well. They spend about $40 a month on clothes and dry goods, $10 on cleaning, $60 on books, and $210 a month on recreation. The total amount they spend on variable factors, including building their home, is $840 a month or $10,000 a year. Their expenses in both fixed and variable categories now total $21,000 a year. Within two years, when the house is finished and the car is paid for, their expenses will drop to $9,000 a year—by more than half. They are, of course, looking forward to that day.

Susan and Doug Taylor

Susan and Doug Taylor have a much smaller house than the Hycliffs. Their house is 800 square feet, in contrast to the 1,900 square foot home the Hycliffs are building. While both started building at the same time, and have incomes that are similar, the Taylors have already completed their house. They have also paid off their cars, so their fixed expenses are quite a bit lower than the Hycliffs'.

The Taylors' fixed expenses total $420 a month or $5,000 a year. This includes $200 a month for food, $100 a month for gas for their two cars, and $60 a month for insurance. It also includes $70 a month for electricity, which includes heating and air conditioning, stove, and water heater.

Partly because the Taylors have been able to reduce their fixed expenses, they spend a disproportionate amount on recreation. Their variable expenses are actually greater than their fixed expenses and total $435 a month or $5,200 a year. This includes monthly expenses of $10 for clothing, $24 for cleaning, $70 for books, and $280 for recreation. That last figure, which works out to $3,360 a year, includes expenses for traveling three months each summer when they are on vacation from their teaching positions. With an income way above their expenses, the Taylors had no idea how much they were spending on recreation until I asked them.

Harold and Mary Englith

Harold and Mary Englith have three children, two teen age boys and one little girl. They are still in the process of completing their

2,000 square foot frame house. The house is three quarters completed and will be worth at least $80,000 when finished. The Engliths have been taking out short-term loans to finish their home and pay $600 a month on these loans. Their other fixed monthly expenses include $300 for groceries for five people, electricity at $35, cooking gas at $6, auto gas at $64, and insurance at $61. Their total fixed expenses come to about $1,100 a month or $13,200 a year. When they are no longer paying $600 a month on their short-term home improvement loans, this amount will drop to $500 a month or $6,000 a year.

The variable expenses for the Englith family include $40 a month for clothes, $40 a month for cleaning, $115 a month for eating out and recreation, and $50 a month for child care. They also give $35 a month in contributions. The total variable expenses come to about $300 a month or $3,600 a year. Together with their fixed expenses, the Englith family spends about $17,000 a year. Once their home is completed, this will drop to about $10,000.

Ways of Saving

By examining the budgets of actual people, we can see how one might save in each of the budget categories. Under housing, Ray Stanley and the Taylors have zero shelter expenses because they own their homes outright. The Englith family saves twenty percent on food because they have a good garden and they keep goats for milk. Ray Stanley saves about sixty percent of his food costs by doing intensive gardening. The most remarkable difference in bills was found under the utilities category, with the Taylors spending $70 a month for an 800 square foot house and the Hycliffs spending only $30 a month for a 1,900 square foot house. The difference occurs because the Hycliffs use gas and the Taylors use electricity. To keep your bills down with an all electric house, you have to use air conditioning and heat very sparingly, which is what Rosa Hunt does. Rosa Hunt also uses an old refrigerator that requires regular defrosting, while Doug and Susan Taylor have a modern frost-free refrigerator. With regard to transportation and insurance costs, there is not much that one can do to save, except to buy used cars and to shop around for insurance.

Under variable expenses one can save by simply deciding not to spend. There is a tendency to spend whatever you have, so when fixed expenses are lowered, the spending on variable items increases. This is undesirable because you end up having no more in savings.

People differed tremendously in the amount they spent on vacations, with the Taylors spending the most and the Engliths managing to spend the least. When Mary Englith takes her children to visit relatives each year, she is certain to travel in someone else's car and to stop at friends' homes along the way. That way she and the children are able to travel across the entire country for under $200.

If you're like most Americans, struggling to survive with an income of over $15,000 a year, you may find the budgets hard to believe. All these budgets are real. While you won't be able to enjoy all the benefits without building your own home in the country, you might benefit from some of our money saving ideas. The next sections will offer advice on how you can save on home living space, entertainment, tools, and heating. I don't attempt to give you detailed descriptions on all these items. I provide only enough so you might judge whether these options are for you.

Homes

People have found that they are able to build by using money that was previously going for rent. Once engaged in building, people found that almost all their resources went into the building of their homes. Most were able to build without getting long term mortgages, but many did find it necessary to take out short-term loans. The majority lived in unfinished houses and used the money they saved from not paying rent to pay back loans or to buy materials to finish their houses.

Building a home while living in it involves many sacrifices. It means that people must live in an unfinished house, often without the amenities we feel are necessary for comfort. Ron and Carol lived with their two children in a home that did not have running water for two years before they were able to install plumbing. Betsy and Hank had to take care of an infant without having water. Judy and I froze the first winter we moved in. When spring arrived, we realized just how open our house was as we watched birds fly into the house.

Entertainment

Once homes are finished, more than construction costs go down. People tend to spend more time on the land and less money on transportation and entertainment. Entertainment for many people means entertaining neighbors at home.

A community center is a natural place to gather in the evening. We post a schedule of events at our community mailbox. I predict that sometime within the next few years we will have a large video screen and be showing films regularly. You can now rent current films for $7 a week, which divided by a hundred people is very reasonable. As the electronics revolution continues, it will become easier to bring the benefits of the city into the countryside.

I look forward to the day when our community hooks into the computer revolution. It would be very realistic for people to get together to buy a micro-computer. Such equipment could be used for entertainment, education, or work. I would love to use a computer for word processing to speed up my writing. The purchase of equipment by the community would be most practical.

Tools

One way for everyone to save a lot of money is by sharing things. Instead of everyone buying tools such as lawn mowers, roto-tillers, and tractors, groups of people can share the expenses and ownership of these tools. When one person buys a tool such as a lawn mower, that person usually buys one of the cheaper machines and then uses it once or twice a month. When people pool their resources, they can buy a quality machine and have it in regular use. Quality machines that are used regularly last longer than cheap machines that sit idle because machines that sit idle have a tendency to rust.

People share all kinds of things; not just tools. Tools are a natural for sharing, especially garden tools and tools that are used in building homes. One radial arm saw has now been used in the construction of over ten homes. The people using these tools don't have any great need for them after their homes are constructed, so the tools get passed on. Another group of things that get passed on are things that people use with babies, such as cradles, bottles, clothes, and toys. One cradle has been used by six families.

Most of the sharing in our community is done very informally, but with a few tools definite rules have been worked out. One such tool is the roto-tiller. In this instance the two individuals who run the roto-tiller for the community charge for its upkeep and their labor. The roto-tiller being discussed in the article below is a large one that an operator rides: it's expensive and tricky to maintain, which is why rules had to be worked out.

21

ROTO-TILLER BACK IN ACTION!!

The roto-tiller engine was recently rebuilt and is now in good running order. Rose and Randy and I spent a sizeable amount of money in the process. We also didn't have the use of the tiller for a good while before we could come up with the money. This prevented us from doing a lot of planting when it needed to be done. Also other people in the co-op weren't able to have their gardens tilled when they needed it done.

After the above experience we have decided to raise the tilling rate to $8 per hour, $4 for the tiller and $4 for the operator. This should provide us with a sizeable maintenance fund to take care of the future needs of the tiller and insure that this valuable tool is available when needed.

If you need some tilling done, contact Rose and Randy or myself.

Thanks, Tom

Most of the time sharing tools works very well, but sometimes there are problems. Problems arise if people don't show respect for other people and their belongings. If someone buys a tool to have it handy when needed, it's upsetting to find it missing because a neighbor took it without checking. I was upset about such an occurrence when I wrote this article in our paper.

A NOTE ON BORROWING THINGS

It's good to share our tools in building a community, but if we don't show some consideration in borrowing, the scene can be ugly. I had just had my land plowed and was in the long process of raking the dead weeds so that I could do some planting when someone took my rake. Several times I came out to the Land hoping to do some raking but was unable to because I had no rake. After three weeks, my rake was returned with a couple of pounds of cement on it. This makes it much less useful to me, because I use the teeth on the rake to dig out roots. What really disturbs me is that a person could be so inconsiderate and take something without checking, keep it for three weeks, and then return it all junked up.

So that people don't get into the habit of doing things like this, I urge the following be practiced in borrowing tools:

1. Check with a person before you take anything.
2. Return things in as good a condition as when you borrowed them, and if you mess something up, clean it. If you break a tool, fix it; and if you can't fix it, replace it.
3. The person borrowing a tool has a duty to return it. A person who loans a tool should not have to chase after the person to whom the

tool is loaned to get the tool back. As soon as a person can return a tool, he or she should do so.

4. No one who borrows a tool from another has a right to loan it to another person without the permission of the owner of the tool.

These suggestions have nothing to do with property rights. They relate to our respecting each other as people. A person buys things so that he or she can have them when needed. Nobody wants to have to go hunting around for tools everytime a job has to be done. We'll all be doing a lot of borrowing from each other, and if we follow a few rules of consideration, our borrowing should have only good results.

Heating

Many people save by using wood for heating and cooking. Putting in wood stoves was one of the first things people did after framing in their homes. Stoves were often purchased in bulk at savings up to thirty percent. Some people started using stoves not only for heating but also for cooking. One enthusiastic member wrote this in our newspaper:

DOWN WITH UTILITY BILLS!!

We finally made the step! We disconnected our electric stove and are living strictly on wood heat and cooking. It's a wonderful experience!

There will be people who still shake their heads and cluck their tongues, but hopefully some day soon they'll also realize the job that can be achieved from a little extra work. We'll have to admit, though, that cooking successfully on a wood stove is acquired only through a good understanding of your stove and the fire and lots and lots of experience.

The food cooked on a wood stove is so much more flavorful. This is because a wood stove oven is airtight, whereas an electric or gas oven has a vent which causes loss of flavor and natural juices. We also learned that because of this airtight oven, the temperature is a great deal hotter, so you'll have to alter your recipes. When the book says you should cook something at 425 degrees, in a wood stove oven 350 degrees or medium heat is sufficient. This is where you'll have to use your own common sense and experiment a lot.

Everyone out here has at least a heating stove. Most stoves are real heating stoves: they are airtight to be effective. One exception is my own, which is a Franklin stove. Franklin stoves are beautiful—when they're open they look like a fireplace—but unfortunately they're never completely sealed. Real heating stoves are airtight with

23

valves to control the air so that burning can be carefully regulated. The difference is that a real heating stove will burn for twelve hours at a time, while I have to get up three times during the night to feed my beautiful stove.

There are a few things to keep in mind when you're installing a stove. First, it's a lot easier to just buy a stove installation kit than to buy all the pieces you need separately. Another thing to consider is that the chimney has to be high enough above the roof or you'll end up with smoke in your house, as we did. A general rule is that the chimney has to be higher than the highest part of your roof. If your stove is in the middle of your house, as mine is, that means that the chimney has to go way above the roof. You also have to have trees cleared away from the chimney so the air can blow the smoke away from your house.

There are problems with wood stoves. On a cold winter day my valley fills with smoke. Here I am, living in the country, and breathing smoke. The problem of smoke only occurs on the coldest days and only for a few hours on those days—so we can tolerate it. But, if we had houses all around us, as they do in the cities, the problem would be intolerable. Wood stoves may be a tremendous help to people in the country, but they are not a solution to the problem of heating homes in densely populated areas. Of course nothing else may be a solution either.

Most people find wood stoves economic and fairly easy to handle. To do it right you should have a rack for wood inside your house that holds all you'll need for a couple of days. That's in case of rain or in case you come down with something and don't feel like going outside for wood. If you have a real heating stove, all you have to do is feed the fire a few times in the evening and once before going to bed. You'll wake up to a nice cozy home, with plenty of embers to start a hot fire in the morning.

For my friend Dave and many other people in the co-op, getting firewood is as much a social activity as it is economic. Several people team together in a truck and go to where they've heard there are oak trees available for the cutting. Often trees are available because a road has just been cleared, land has been leveled for a shopping center, or trees have fallen for natural reasons. Several people can pool the expenses for a chain saw and gas for a truck and get free firewood.

I prefer to just buy firewood. Where I live it's very cheap. A man will deliver a half cord of wood for $50, and that's enough to take me through the season. The wood is seasoned oak, cut into eighteen to twenty-four inch pieces (just right for my stove), and is split. Mainly I buy firewood because the man I buy it from has a machine that splits it, which makes a lot more sense than doing the splitting by hand. My friend who gathers firewood admits that it's actually more sensible to buy firewood when you consider the cost of a chain saw, the time and work gathering wood and splitting it, and how cheaply you can purchase wood, but he says he likes the whole idea of going with a group for wood.

SAVING
WAYS OF

CHAPTER
◆ FOUR ◆

SAVING ON HOME CONSTRUCTION

T here are many ways of getting a house. A person does not have to do all the construction in order to save. Hopefully, this chapter will give you some idea of the many options that exist and the many ways that you can save on home construction.

Paying for Your Land

I don't think anyone should buy land in the country unless they're planning to use it within five years or so of buying it. It makes no sense to be making land payments for a long time without getting something for your money. The money you pay will mostly go into interest, which is really money paid for using the land, not for purchasing it. Since this point is confusing to many people, I will explain it here.

In our co-operative, individuals bought their acres of land (complete with common land and development money) for $2,700 an acre. Financing was arranged so individuals had to put only $200 down and pay ten percent interest on the balance. Monthly payments were only $35, $20.83 of which went for interest and $14.17 of which went for the principal. Today, land in my area would cost $5,000 an acre and interest might be fifteen percent. Suppose you were to buy land with a $500 down payment at $5,000 an acre at fifteen percent interest and paid $65 a month. Your first month the interest portion would be $56.25 and only $8.75 would go toward reducing your debt. If you held your land for ten years without using it, this would cost you $7,800 in payments and you would still owe $2,092. Your land would have cost you almost twice the original amount. You might have been better off saving until you had the cash to buy the land outright. Of course, then you would be taking a chance that there might be no land in the community left and also inflation might put the price of land out of reach. Even with these two considerations, I'd still advise people not to buy land unless they are going to use it within five years.

Most people got tremendous use of their land right from the start. One couple with children put their $200 down, and with another $200 built a small one-room building and started living on their land. From that point on the hundreds of dollars that had been going into rent were turned toward buying materials for their house. They built one room after another in a flexible modular design. Now they have a very nice home with no mortgage.

In an intentional community you can live cheaply because no one will complain about your lifestyle. You have freedom you can't get elsewhere. It is different than when someone tries to live in a tiny building in a normal neighborhood. All the neighbors would get up in arms over property values. In an alternate community people want their property values and taxes to be low. They are building homes to live in, not to sell. The people in your co-op community will end up with large, beautiful, creative, energy efficient homes—because that is what most people like to live in. But at the beginning people will live in some small structures, many of which will eventually be workshops and barns, and people will often live in large homes when they are nothing but shells with studs showing in the walls.

I would advise people to move out any way they can as soon as they can. Get out from under paying rent. If you already own a house in the city, rent it and use the money you were paying the bank to help build your home in the country. A tip, though, if you decide to live in your house while building it: I advise that you completely finish a section of your house, live in it, and build out from there. Otherwise, you can end up crawling over your belongings and spend more time moving things around than you spend building.

I was living on my land within two years of purchasing it. During the first year I used the land for picnicking and put up an 8 × 16 foot shed that today is the study I'm working in right now. Next to my land, that shed was the best buy I ever made. I bought it as a used prefabricated storage building for $40. It gave me a place to run electric wires to, and the fuse box I put in it now serves my entire house. That shelter was used for storing my belongings when I traveled, was a place for camping and entertaining, and was a place for storing and running the tools I used in building my house.

Building a Shed

An 8 × 16 or smaller shed is easy to build. You can use concrete blocks for the foundation. Lay two sixteen foot long 4 × 4s parallel on the blocks. Make sure they are parallel by measuring diagonally from the tip of one to the other—the measurement should be the same. To level the pieces all you need is a carpenter's level which you place first on one of the 4 × 4s (the higher one). The low end can be lifted up with scrap pieces of lumber until it's just about right. To make it exact use wooden shingles. To line up the second 4 × 4 at the same height as the first, just put the level on a 2 × 4 between the two 4 × 4s.

After the 4 × 4s are in place run 2 × 4s across them one foot apart. These should be anchored with hurricane clips, which also holds them nicely in place. Now you can put sheets of plywood down for the floor. For extra strength you should run these sheets perpendicular to the 2 × 4s. Once the floor is in you have a platform to work on.

A nice simple design for a shed is to have a simple shed roof, which you get by having one wall lower than the other. One wall of my 8 × 16 study is twelve feet high, the other, ten feet. For framing the walls remember that every sixteen inches there has to be a stud, and for windows and doors you need headers—pieces above these openings that distribute the weight.

The roof can be made with ten foot 2 × 6s. You should anchor these with hurricane clips. You might top this with pieces of plywood and put tar paper over the plywood. If you want to insulate the shed, the easiest way is to use 1½ inch thick styrofoam that is cut ten feet by two feet. Hold it in place with 1 × 2 furring strips. I covered the layer of styrofoam with tar paper again: the trick of preventing leaks is to use many layers of tar paper. Then, for my final protection against the rain, I nailed 2 × 10 foot sheets of aluminum roofing to the furring strips.

The combination of furring strips, styrofoam, tar paper, and aluminum roofing works really well—I used this combination on both my shed and my house. Styrofoam is an excellent insulator; it's better than fiberglass, and it's a lot easier to work with. Fiberglass consists of little pieces of glass that have a nasty way of getting into both your skin and lungs. It's especially bad when you have to install it under a roof while working on a ladder. While it's not good to breathe the bits of styrofoam that are released when you cut it, this danger is minimized when you buy styrofoam pre-cut.

Electrical Service

I paid an electrician to install the fuse box and service equipment on my shed. He charged only $120 for installing 100 amp. service: 200 amps. would have been almost twice as much. Many of my neighbors installed power poles for construction and then installed service equipment again after they had framed in their house. I think it's a waste to put in temporary service only to replace it later. I also think that there isn't enough saved by putting in service yourself for it to be worth the effort. It could end up costing you more because some of the piping is extremely expensive and hard to cut properly. But who am I to stop you?

Know Your Land Before You Build

It's a good idea to spend a lot of time on your land before you start building your home. Get the feel of it. Try a few locations in your mind until you have the one that's just right. Nowadays, with the emphasis on using the sun, many good books detail the placing of a house. Most of these have the living areas to the south because they will receive five times as much heat in the winter that way. A five foot roof overhang will shade the same rooms in the summer. You might have your house just slightly off this north/south setting to insure that mildew doesn't develop on walls that are totally unreached by the sun. The actual plan should combine knowledge of solar construction, the lay of your land, and your own background, concerns, and interest.

I'm a Northerner by background, and so the season I hate the most in the South is the summer. I figured that the main problem would be keeping my house cool. You can always burn firewood to heat a home, but there is no renewable fuel you can use to cool a house. So I chose an acre at the bottom of a valley, because a valley is cooler than a hill, and built my house under the shade of several large trees. The ceilings in my house are high—from ten to sixteen feet—and the house has a shed roof with windows at the top. I wrote an article in our paper about the design of my house which I share with you here.

THIS IS A HOT ISSUE!!

Solving the HOT BALLS Problem

Imagine that air consists of lots of balls. Some of these balls are hot and some are cold, and the hot ones rise to the top. The normal house (where Norm and Norma live) has a bad case of hot balls. As the air outside gets hotter more and more hot balls get trapped, which heats up Norm and Norma.

To fix this "hot balls problem" the roof needs to be set up so that the hot balls get pushed off the edge. To do this a shed roof is best and it is also best to have an opening at the very top.

I figure that my balls will be nice and cold with this design, . . . and if that doesn't work I'll take a cold shower.

Four Ways to Get a House

One thing wrong with the popular pioneer books on dropping out is that they present people with an all or nothing choice: you're either going to rot away in a city or you have to do everything for yourself in the country. After reading such books, people who have no carpentry experience feel that building a home is beyond them. Actually your choices are very broad, and you can have the degree of involvement in procuring your home that you desire. These are your options:

1. Move a house.
2. Be the contractor.
3. Build with a buddy.
4. Do part or all yourself.

Move a House

Moving a house is an option you should at least consider. You could end up with a fine, custom finished, large home for under $10,000. One couple purchased a 1,200 square foot house for $2,000, moved it for $2,600, and fixed it up with $5,000 worth of materials. They hired labor for many jobs because they were both busy working in town; but if they had done everything themselves, their total cost would have been under $10,000.

To find a house, check newspaper ads under homes for sale: sometimes an ad reads "house to move." That's how my neighbors found their home. If you don't see an ad, check with house moving contractors—they usually know of several homes that are available. Still another source is to check areas where urban renewal (more accurately—urban removal) is going on. You can often get houses for a nominal fee. It's cheaper for a developer to give a house away than it is to demolish a house. Beautiful homes do get demolished, which is a waste of all the energy and materials that went into building them. You're doing everyone a service when you recycle an old house.

You'll want to look over an old home very carefully before buying it. Check under the foundation by climbing under the house. Take a chisel with you and don't be afraid to cut into the wood to inspect for dry rot and termites. Have a carpenter go with you to check the sills and floor system. Go into the attic and examine for rot under the roof. Go over the house carefully and do whatever you must to check it out thoroughly. Bring twenty friends with you and jump all over the house.

The real trick with moving a house is to visualize possibilities beyond the ugly external features. Separate what is important, such as the foundation, from what is not. Keep in mind that what you want is basically a frame that you can finish the way you like. Don't worry about anything that you're planning to change anyway. Broken glass, stains on the walls, a stupid floor plan—none of these things should bother you if you're planning to put up new siding and knock out some walls. To figure out if a wall can be changed you have to see if it's a load bearing wall—someone with carpentry knowledge can tell this. If you don't know any carpenters, hire one to tell you which walls can be changed.

The actual moving of a house is the simplest part. Contractors charge about $2 a square foot. Distance is not a major factor. An extra cost is incurred if utility or traffic control wires have to be disconnected, in which case you would be charged about $100 for each wire. A single story house should present no problems because a man stands on top of the house and lifts wires over it. It's quite a sight to see someone dancing over roof rafters with a long pole in their hand, lifting the live wires over your rooftop. This is a dangerous and difficult job. But don't worry—you don't have to do it yourself.

To minimize trouble with utility wires, my neighbors took the roof down by removing the roof rafters and laying the gable ends on their sides. It took eight people to hold the gables and put them down gently. This, of course, calls for a party.

Your house can move over roads you wouldn't want to drive on. The house mover's truck has a clearance of four feet, so it can go over a pasture. What this means is that you can put a house just about anywhere. The only major consideration is big trees. You need a clear path the width of your house. A reputable contractor will check the route with you and set up the foundation of the new house.

If you get a good buy, for under $5,000 you could have a 1,200 square foot home moved to your land. As soon as it arrives, its value triples, and you can borrow money from a bank for home improvement. Now, instead of paying rent, your money will go into improving your own home.

If your house is in rough shape, you may want to gut it—knock all the plaster out and clean it so that the studs show. It took two people three days to gut the 1,200 square foot house. Once down to the studs, you can wire the house, put in your own plumbing, and add insulation. From then on all the work is on things that will change the permanent appearance. Since you put so little money into getting a framed house, you might want to put more into the finishing touches.

Some things to keep in mind in moving a house are that you have to check a house very carefully before buying, and you should check a contractor carefully before hiring one. There's a big difference between house moving contractors. Ask a contractor for references—people whose houses he's moved. Make sure the contractor takes care of providing you with a new foundation. Check all these things before you move the house. Another thing you might want to do before moving a house is to fumigate it. My friends moved their house complete with mice and cockroaches.

One advantage of moving a house is that you end up with a house right away. Your front end costs are small, and you can get your money back by getting a home improvement loan. You'll end up with a quality home by this route—many of the old homes are built of heart pine from virgin forests. Some disadvantages include the limitations on the floor plan built into the old structure and the fact that you cannot really make an old house as energy efficient as a new one. Another factor to consider is the element of risk—the house could fall apart. You can negotiate insurance with the mover. Most movers are bonded and insured, so they retain financial liability during the move. All risks are less if you make sure you get a reputable house mover who will check the house carefully before moving it.

Be the Contractor

You can be involved in the construction of your home and save money, without doing any of the physical work yourself, by being a contractor. A contractor lines up and supervises the work of the individual subcontractors. This involves lining up someone to help you with the plans, or doing the plans yourself, and then hiring the independent workers, perhaps people living in the land co-op, who will do the separate jobs such as framing the house in, plastering, plumbing, electrical, etc. By doing this, you cut out all the professional contractor's profits, and you can also save money assisting the people you hire. I hired a couple of co-op members to work as carpenters and spent many happy hours as their assistant. That way I could take advantage of their expertise yet still be involved in building my own home.

Building with a Buddy

Many people on the land co-op buddied up on building houses, with people from two households building two homes together. Construction work goes more quickly and certainly more pleasantly when two friends work together. People can pool their knowledge, and with people building all around you, you can easily look at what your neighbors are doing to know what the next step is. After one house is completed, everyone moves in, so you can all live on the land while completing the second house. Just be sure that everyone understands whose house is to be completed first and that everyone is duty-bound to complete the second house.

Do Part or All Yourself

There are any number of options on building a house because you can do any amount of the work you want by yourself rather than by hiring people. Some jobs are easier than others, and some of the easiest jobs are also the most costly. I did not know anything at all about construction, yet I was able to put the foundation in by myself, checking with neighbors for advice only a few times. As I describe the various stages in the construction of a house, I will indicate the things that an unskilled person can do. There are also some things that can be done by many people together at a work party. Just put up a sign, provide beer, and encourage neighbors to come over for these tasks.

Post & Beam Construction

There are two main types of construction for wood frame homes: post and beam construction and story-by-story construction. I'll discuss a third type, dome construction, later. With post and beam construction, you have large posts, either square or like telephone poles, going from the ground up to the roof. The house plan is worked around these posts, with maybe one post in the middle of the living room. With story-by-story construction you build a platform—the first story floor—then walls which will hold the second story. Then you build the second story floor, which is held up by those walls, and on you go for as many levels as you want. Each type of construction has its advantages and disadvantages.

With post and beam construction you have to spend a lot of money at the very first stage, which is sinking huge beams into the ground. One of my neighbors spent $2,000 for this in comparison to the $800 I spent to the point of having a finished floor. After the posts are in the ground, work goes very fast with post and beam, and you can quickly have a rough frame with a roof. The roof insures that you are protected from rain as you work on the house. In contrast, with balloon construction, the wood gets wet constantly as you are working; and to avoid getting wet yourself, you lose many construction days. One advantage that post and beam has is that after the initial stage, it allows tremendous flexibility for building in stages. You can start with half of your third floor and finish the second and first floor later or do the work in any order you wish. With story-by-story construction you have to put in all the levels until you get to the roof. Since my house is only one story, I decided on story-by-story construction; but I think that if I wanted more levels, I would have preferred post and beam.

Most of the homes in our community that were built with post and beam construction were built by individuals who are carpenters or individuals who hired carpenters. Post and beam construction involves much more than balloon construction. First, holes have to be dug for the beams, which go at least six feet into the ground. Digging the holes is best done using a machine called an auger; it is definitely not a job one person would want to do alone with a shovel. Then huge poles have to be put into place, another job that is best done by machine. After the poles are in place someone has to climb up the posts and notch them so they will hold horizontal beams. Then the horizontal beams that will hold up the ceiling and the floors have to be lifted into place. These are not jobs that I would advise for an amateur; it is no accident that no amateurs attempted this type of construction in our community.

Story-by-Story Construction

The basic idea of story-by-story construction is that you put short posts into the ground that hold up a floor which is from three to six feet above the ground. Without any prior construction experi-ence I was able to put in a floor. It wasn't much harder than putting in a floor for the shed that I already described.

Once the floor is in, your house is ready for framing. I hired help at this point because experienced carpenters know ways of tying the entire building together. Framing goes very fast, so you won't have time to make decisions if you hire help. I had two fellows waiting on me for a few hours while I tried to decide where to put a window. The person doing the framing should be provided with very clear drawings showing where the doors and windows will be. After the house is framed you can once again do jobs yourself. I list below all the jobs required to build a house and indicate the jobs that you can do yourself, the jobs that you might organize a work party to do, and the jobs you might want to hire help for.

Chart of Jobs Required to Build a House

Task	Do Yourself	Work Party	Hire Help
Dig holes	*	*	
Put in 6' posts	*		
Level posts	*		
Put up sills	*		*
Run joists	*		*
Put down flooring	*		
Frame walls			*
Put sheathing on roof	*	*	
Put up siding	*	*	
Electrical wiring	*		*
Plumbing	*		*
Put dry wall up	*		*
Plastering			*
Nail wall boards	*		
Put in windows, trim			*
Kitchen cabinets (cheap type)	*		
Kitchen cabinets custom			*
Shingles, tin	*	*	

You will benefit in a dozen ways from being in a land co-operative when it comes to building your home. I never would have been able to build a home if it weren't in a loving community. The fact that people were building all around me was an inspiration and a source of knowledge. I would examine the other houses and see what happens at each stage. When I was building and needed help and advice, people were always willing. Neighbors helped cut the posts for my foundation. I was able to hire neighbors to help me frame the house and, because they were my good neighbors, I could trust them to work when they wanted to and to keep track of their own hours. When we had walls framed that were too heavy for us to lift, neighbors would give us a hand, and we helped others also. Some people had siding parties, and roofing parties, at which a dozen neighbors helped individuals finish their homes. A group of women formed a collective to come to the aid of a woman who was building a home. The women's collective shingled this lady's roof and helped in other ways. The net result was that many people ended up with beautiful homes at a cost that is hard to believe. Some very fine homes were put up for less than $10,000. Should the government ever get serious about low cost housing, I think they will want to examine the land co-op approach.

Domes

Domes are composed out of triangles. Those triangles are of, at most, three different sizes, so dome construction becomes a project for mass production of triangular sections. Because domes are so adaptable to mass production, several companies produce dome kits. These kits, for the most part, are ideal for small camping shelters and greenhouses; but the domes you can make with them are not large enough for permanent homes. If you want to live in a dome, you have to build from scratch.

Dome construction is for those who like exacting work. The parts have to be made just the right size or they won't go together. Precision is needed because of what happens at the final stages of dome construction. When you put the triangles together into a dome, you start at the bottom and work toward the crown. Everything goes easily until you get near the top. Then it gets harder and harder to fit the pieces in. If the parts were not cut just right, the last pieces won't fit.

To cut pieces accurately you'll have to use a radial arm saw. Before cutting all the pieces, and taking a chance on cutting them all wrong, you might want to make a small model. The angles will be the same, no matter what the size of the dome.

Ways to Get Building Materials

There are as many alternative ways to getting building materials as there are ways of obtaining a home. Some of my neighbors scavenged around construction sites to get discarded plywood and studs which they used to build a shed that housed two adults and two children for two years. Their total cost was under $100. I tore down tobacco barns and built my house largely out of lumber that cost me almost nothing. I have twenty-five foot long 6 × 6 rough hewn beams running through my living room. These are complemented with beautiful barn siding on the walls. Another option is doing demolition of old houses or buildings slated to be torn down. I got all the doors and even some bathroom fixtures from buildings that were demolished. Still another option, if you have the money, is to buy your materials new. You can save considerably by buying large quantities with your neighbors, and can also save by taking advantage of contractors' discounts which lumber companies will often give to individuals who are building houses.

Tearing Down Barns

Back in 1973 I earned my living by tearing down tobacco barns and selling the lumber. The co-op had just started, and several of us went to work tearing down a barn to get lumber for our homes. Then I decided to set up a lumber yard to sell some of the lumber and aluminum roofing to offset gas costs. From there I ended up with a business. My mode of operation was to buy a barn and offer fellow co-op members half the lumber for taking the barn down. As my part of the bargain, I paid for the barn and trucked their half of the lumber to their homesites. The business worked all right, except that I couldn't get enough barns to keep it going. After counting 700 barns in the local area, I thought there was a plentiful supply, but it turned out that most of the barns were owned by huge lumber companies that didn't want to be bothered with selling them. They preferred to just let the buildings rot, rather than take any chances with liability or inconvenience to themselves.

There are both advantages and disadvantages with using barn wood on homes. The advantage is that the wood, which is often from virgin forests, has been dried over a long period of time. It is hard to drive nails into the wood, but once a nail is in it stays in. A building inspector examining my house told me that my house was made of rift wood. I told him that there was nothing wrong with the wood, and he then explained what rift wood is. When pine has more than seventeen rings per inch, it is considered to be as strong as oak and is given a special name, "rift wood."

On the other hand, barn wood presents problems for building. First, you won't get most of the type of lumber you need to build a house from tearing down barns. Barns are made of 1 × 4s and 4 × 4s, which are good for framing walls, of 6 × 6s, which are good for beams, but they have almost no 2 × 6s, which you need for joists, or planking for floors and ceiling. It's problematic whether you want to use barn siding for the side of your house. Pine rots after a while, so I used cypress, which is much more resistant. I'd say that I got less than a third of the lumber for my house out of barns, but some of the lumber I got is so pretty that I have no regrets about my work.

One thing you might be able to get off barns is aluminum roofing. Aluminum on a roof will last twenty years or more, whereas shingles last only ten years. From every sensible viewpoint, aluminum roofing is best. Unfortunately, aluminum is often confused with tin, which is cheaper and rusts. When I had my house appraised, the appraiser wrote that I had a tin roof and decreased the value of the house. He agreed that aluminum is the very best kind of roof but said that since mostly poor houses have that type of roof, it subtracts from the value of a house.

In case you want a barn for the lumber as well, I'll share some trade secrets with you. First, you should set up some safety ropes so that the barn doesn't fall on you when you're only half way through with demolition. Second, you will want to avoid breakage. You want the siding to land softly in sections, so you can use it on your walls. The best way to do this is to have the sides land on a pile of rubber tires.

Some barns have special features like large barn doors. I'd advise taking them off very carefully and using them whole as sections of paneling in a house. Don't do as I did. I piled things up figuring that I'd ship them out later, and they rotted in the meantime. When you have something ready to use, move it out to where you're going to use it.

After tearing down the barns I stopped worrying about saving every board foot and worked out some ways to get a lot of usable wood fast. We dropped sections of the barns at a time and cut the wood with a chain saw when it was on the ground. Rather than pulling nails, we just cut the sections between the beams. This provided us with ten foot 2 × 4s that had no nails in them, rather than twelve foot pieces with nails.

The equipment you will need for tearing down a barn includes a small gas chain saw, wrecking bars (similar to crow bars), and a flatbed truck. My feelings are mixed on tearing down barns. It was a lot of work for the small amount of usable wood, and it was very dangerous. Two fellows in our community were on top of a barn when it collapsed, and it was miraculous that neither was seriously hurt. I was in the middle of a barn when it went down and barely made it through the side of the barn before it collapsed like a scissors.

Demolition

Still another possibility is to get materials from buildings that are slated to be demolished. I went to an auction at a motel that was slated to come down and walked away the proud owner of several heavy wooden doors at $7 each, a toilet at $5 and a bathtub at $20. Three days of hard work later I was still trying to remove the bathtub: I had no idea it was set in solid cement. Well, I finally got it out after putting a few scratches in it and moved it to my land. Several neighbors helped me move the four hundred pound monster into the house. After a year in the house and after I had tried painting it several times to cover the scratches, my wife insisted that I remove the monster. My neighbors once again came to the rescue. Then all I had left was an ugly toilet that we could never quite clean and some very fine doors. I'd recommend that the only thing you get from a demolition auction is doors. Ours are fine, and since I re-painted the one in the living room, it no longer says that checkout time is one p.m.

CHAPTER
• FIVE •

PRODUCING YOUR OWN FOOD

M any people produce a good portion of their food, and many others trade for food within the community. People have the security of knowing that they are eating wholesome, organically grown food and that their supply of this food cannot be disrupted by a gas shortage. I won't attempt to provide details on gardening and raising livestock. There are enough books on that, and we haven't the space here. I only provide enough information on our experiences so that you can decide whether growing vegetables and raising livestock might interest you.

The Joys of Gardening

Many of us are out here so we can grow our own food organically. While gardening is certainly part of how to live comfortably on a poverty budget, gardening has spiritual benefits as great as its economic benefits. Members of our community have written of the joys of gardening.

On Vegetables

Little green things have sprouted all over the land—shortly many of them will be edible and could supply all of us with the vitamins and minerals needed for optimum health. Five years ago many of us thought we would be producing all or most of our own food by now— shows you how little we knew. But I reckon that's to be expected in a society which promotes the once-a-week shopping to save time and energy at the expense of our health. The ancients and wiser people of our time know that food right out of the ground (except for certain roots which should be cured) holds its own special magic. Daily marketing which occurs in other countries is one way to get fresh produce; growing your own is probably the best; bartering for or buying it from

45

neighbors is another. If one holds the belief that "time is money," vegetables can end up being pretty expensive, but if viewed as an integral part of a preventive wholistic health plan, getting fresh produce is well worth it.

In our community, at this time, we are not all able to spend the time required to grow most of our food. Some of us are tending fruit and nut trees and vines which will not produce for years to come, but one day! Some plant a spring garden; others grow food all year long. The important thing is that we are a growing community in more ways than one, and we can provide a lot for each other if we make the connections and take the time.

We've learned about gardening by trial and error. An early pioneer, Tom, had this to report in our community paper.

AND SOW IT GROWS . . .

If I had planted early enough, not only would I have been eating a lot sooner, but I wouldn't have suffered as much insect damage. Insects seem to get worse as the summer progresses. If I had found a way to keep the rabbits out, I would have had soybeans and Swiss chard. I've tried all kinds of things to keep rabbits out but no luck. I put tin around the bottom of my fence, but I guess they're climbing over it or something. I even tried spreading blood meal around but that didn't help either. I guess what you need is a tight chicken wire fence, especially if you plan to grow soybeans. Rabbits won't touch anything else if there are soybeans around. I planted two crops and both were eaten completely.

Right now the rabbits are doing some trimming on my peanuts and pole beans, and they ate a row of Swiss chard when they first ran out of soybeans.

I never thought I would be chasing cardinals away, but they really love sunflowers. Bean beetles seem misnamed to me—they much prefer gourds to beans. The way it looks I may not get any gourds as the beetles destroy the flowers and fruits. I guess I can forget my dreams of an infinite supply of peanuts to munch on, too. My peanut plants are just up and dying for no real obvious reason, although their root systems seem to be very weak, so I guess they have nematodes on their roots. I won't even try to describe the fungus that grows in ears of corn, but it is one of the grossest things I have ever seen. Water is the one thing which didn't find its way into my garden often enough. It's been a very dry summer, and I don't think my garden would have made it at all if it hadn't been fairly well mulched.

Well, enough of the hassles. There's nothing to compare to the pleasure of eating fresh vegetables from your own garden. Fresh pickled sweet corn is just too good to be true. Watching things grow or looking up at a 12 foot sunflower plant with a 1 foot diameter head, while a humming bird feeds on its nectar is enough for me. You don't have to have Mexican weeds to get high from growing things.

Rose and Randy reported better luck.

WE'RE GROWING

It's a joy to plant a seed and watch it grow—we've planted many and they're flourishing. We had the same experience last year and were surprised by it, considering it was a first year garden in the middle of a field with water being hauled from the trailer in 55 gallon drums. We weren't prepared to eat it all, and we didn't—much of it simply returned from whence it came. But a year later things are different!

There's a well here now, and there're animals who are just crazy about the food we're growing, but most important there's you who are purchasing food of questionable age and quality in stores or at stands. We would like to share some time and conversation while picking food right here in our garden so that you can preserve as many vitamins, minerals, and good feelings as possible. Barter is beautiful (it works out here on the land real well), and a supplement for our income would certainly help.

Right now we have spinach, Swiss chard, bibb and leaf lettuce, English peas, broccoli, cauliflower. We will have cabbage very soon, and then we are hoping for a good crop of beans and squash of various types, tomatoes, eggplant, and corn. Stop by our garden when you're out at the land and help us enjoy it.

In July, we'll be starting plants in the cabbage family and biennials and perennials of daisy, Sweet William, carnation, pansy, and hollyhocks for fall planting. If you would like us to start some for you, please let us know.

The most important thing about gardening, besides preparing your soil and having a good chicken wire fence, is knowing when to plant. To get the maximum benefit from your garden you want to harvest food when you need it. Often you will have more than you need of an item, so you will also want to know how to prepare items like squash many different ways so you don't get too tired of them. A garden has a neutral season. Spring planting and harvesting are easy enough, but if you want to have your garden produce more than once a year, you have to be active during the summer when the spring plants are harvested. Rose wrote of some things to do during the summer harvest to extend the productivity of your garden.

Now that there's some empty space in the garden where the early spring crops were, it's a good time to prepare for the planting of soybeans. Soybeans can be eaten green, dry roasted, or dried for use in soaps, loaves, breads and vegetarian protein dishes. Making tofu or soybean curd is an easy process also.

Seeds can be planted in July for summer annuals such as balsam, celosia, marigold, morning glory and SUNFLOWERS. It's also a good time to plant summer-flowering bulbs, rhizomes and tubers-caladiums, cannasa, dahlias, spider lilies and galdiolus. Daylilies are at their best right now. They're good to eat, too, in soups and salads.

There are at least two growing seasons, Spring and Fall. Rose wrote of things that can be planted in September.

IT'S TIME TO START GROWING

September and early October is the time for planting cabbage, broccoli, cauliflower, Brussels sprouts, Chinese cabbage, collards, mustards, turnips, rutabaga, beets, carrots, parsnips, lettuce, spinach and Swiss chard.

We experimented with pinto, black and navy beans this spring and found that they should have something to climb on. If these beans are planted now, a good crop might be harvested before frost. We're experimenting this fall with Wando peas which are supposed to be heat tolerant, bush sweet peas.

Rose writes of the late Fall that,

Actually most of the garden work now is really geared toward preparation for the Spring garden—collecting manure and mulch and planting green manure crops. Coarse seeded winter rye is one of the best nonleguminous cover crops. If planted now, frost will not check its growth so it may be cut every 2–3 weeks during the winter to provide a lot of organic matter.

Clover, of course, is the best green manure as it produces nitrogen as well as organic matter. Its seed is also the most costly; but when one considers that a good clover crop turned under can add 150 lbs. of actual nitrogen to the soil per acre (equivalent to approximately 5 tons of manure), it's definitely worth it.

Rose

Chickens

It's not always economical to raise chickens, but you may want to raise them to insure that you're eating wholesome food. Chicken feed no longer can be bought for chicken feed, so dollar for dollar it may cost more to raise chickens than to buy eggs and meat in the store. This might change, and there are more reasons for raising chickens than saving money, so you might want to know what is involved in raising chickens anyway.

Chickens are prone to many special problems, including disease and cannibalism. Rose reported on a case of cannibalism in chickens in our paper.

A CASE OF CANNIBALISM IN CHICKENS

The day finally arrived when we were to pick up our chickens. Much mystery and excitement surrounded the whole venture, as we had had twenty-one days to speculate on the outcome of our experiment. It had taken us eleven days to collect ninety-six eggs from our flock. Storing them in our refrigerator, there was room for little else, and trying to sex them by shape (long, thin ones are cockrals supposedly) was a hit or miss affair since most of them were medium-sized, uniformly oval-looking. The incubator was warmed up, after a few weeks the eggs were turned, and finally they were put in the basket in preparation for their hatching. But we had not given our flock a breeder ration nor was there any way to know the outcome of the mating of our Rhode Island Red rooster to our five-breed-hen flock, so we had some misgivings.

But when we opened the door to the incubator, our doubts vanished. Thirty-five chicks the first day—black, yellow, brown and numerous shades thereof! The second day found us with sixty-four beautiful-looking, healthy chicks.

We kept them indoors for two days as much for our benefit as theirs—an eight-month old with a fist full of chick and a grin to match is quite a sight! On the third day they were moved into a biddie box made especially for them, and all seemed well.

On the fourth day, one chick was dead, her insides pulled out by the others, and two more had bloody vents. The next day we had an epidemic of cannibalism. According to Jerome Belanger in The Homesteader's Handbook to Raising Small Livestock, *some of the causes of cannibalism are "crowding, boredom, too much heat, too much light and improper diet." Another text claims that it can be inherited, while another says that the reason for it simply is not known. Each book suggested one or two possible remedies, and we tried four with good results.*

First we added cornmeal and then extra salt to their ration. Then we built extra feeders in an attempt to provide spacious feeding areas. We also clipped off ⅓ of their beaks, and finally we built an enclosed area on the ground so they could scratch around in the dirt. We feel that this more than anything helped the situation because while it didn't provide a lot more space, it did offer them a more natural, interesting environment. Also, as soon as we saw any evidence of picking, we separated those chicks from the rest to allow the wound to heal. We noted that at first the picking centered around the vent, then the neck, and finally on the back and breast as the pin feathers began to appear. The chicks outgrew their picking after two long weeks of hourly checking for casualties. But it was all well worth it as we now have a flock of plump, pretty young hens who we hope will lay lots and lots of pretty brown eggs!

Rose

Goats

Goats are extremely popular with people in our community. Part of the reason for their popularity is that the lives of goats become intermeshed with those of humans. Goats have been bred so long that they are ill-adapted to living without human intervention. The intervention is now necessary because if they were on their own, they would harm each other fighting over their mother's milk and would also hurt their mothers. They are dependent on humans at every stage of their development.

Human intervention in the lives of goats starts when the kids are no longer allowed to nurse their mothers at one and one-half months old. Various methods are used to feed the goats after this period. Some people separate the kids from their mother immediately and feed the kids from a bottle, so the kids will never associate milk with their mother's teats. Instead of letting the goats feed directly, they milk the goats, put the milk in bottles, and then they feed the kids. Seems like a few extra steps, doesn't it? But the alternative is to have trouble later on when you want to have the mother's milk for yourself. Paul let his goats nurse on their mother and then had trouble when he found that the goats wouldn't accept the bottle.

It may seem cruel to separate the kids from their mothers. It seemed cruel to Diann, so she devised a method so that the kids could be with their mother without nursing. Her method involves dressing the mother in a T-shirt with the shirt pinned up over the udders. When the kids tried to get milk, they couldn't find a way to get any, so they concluded that milk is produced in bottles. The kids were able to be with their mother, and Diann was able to have the mother's milk.

Feeding goat kids from bottles is as hard as feeding human kids the same way. The bottles have to be sterilized, etc. At first you feed the kids their mother's milk, which at the time of giving birth is a darker, more yellow liquid called milk colostrum. It's good for the kids because it has antibodies and nutrients, and the kids shouldn't be denied that for at least two and a half months. Then what you feed the goats is gradually changed. First they get their mother's milk, then reconstituted dry milk, and then a special artificial milk that's cheap and has vitamins that are special for goats. My neighbors advise feeding the kids five times a day at first, then tapering off to three times a day, twice a day, etc. If that sounds like a lot of work—feeding goats from sterilized bottles five times a day—you're right.

One neighbor who has no time for taking care of kids avoids using bottles entirely by separating the mother goat from her kids except for brief periods. Mother and child reunion is under controlled circumstances because otherwise the kids can hurt the mother by grabbing her teats too greedily. If left alone the kids would also hurt each other as they fought over mother for udder delight.

After taking care of the kids you might become attached to them; they will certainly become attached to you. To become even closer, you might stroke their teats every once in a while, so they'll get used to having your hands on them. Once you start milking them, you'll get even closer.

To do the milking you will want to have the proper equipment. You should have a milking stool and a bucket that is made for milking—one with a crescent shaped opening on top that protects against getting foreign material in the milk.

My neighbors recommend these procedures. Hold the bucket so that nothing can fall into it. Use a wet cloth to rub the udders before taking milk. Throw out the first squirt because the first milk contains the most bacteria, and then squirt as much as you can get into the bucket. You should, of course, have set things up so that the goat is busy eating. If all goes well, you should be able to get a quart and a half in three minutes, and you can do this twice a day. Tina has two goats and reports that it takes her ten minutes to milk both.

You may wonder what goat keepers do with male goats. I asked the same question one day as I was eating stew at my neighbor's house. I remembered that they had a male goat named Zeke that I hadn't seen for a few days. After chewing through a rather tough piece of stew, I asked what happened to male goats. I was informed that I was eating Zeke stew. He was one tough old goat.

Goats require some health care. They require medicine for tetanus and worming. Most of the medicines you can buy cheaply from a farm supply store. Tina reports that it cost her $25 a year for five goats, but some of the medicines you'll have to buy from a veterinarian. Also, after giving them worm tablets you will have to take samples of the goat's droppings to the vet. Tina reports that the most pleasant way to do this, or I should say the least unpleasant, is to handy-wrap the little pieces and then place them in the refrigerator. Don't worry about how they will look. They'll look like little chocolate candies. In fact that's what Gerry thought they were when he went to the refrigerator for a snack.

I'm not sure what the fascination is with goats. Maybe they're popular because they are such efficient milk machines. A female drops her kids at the ripe age of one year old. After her second litter at two years old, she approaches her prime milk production, which peaks at five years old. From two years on, a goat can produce three gallons of milk a day. When you consider the size of goats and that they eat cheap foods, that is indeed efficient production. But the fascination goes beyond economics. Goats are extremely individual animals with lots of odd quirks. They won't ever step in a puddle, in mud, or get their feet wet in any other way. They have a definite hierarchy. If you milk them in a certain order and then try to change the order, you'll hurt their feelings. If you try to add some guest goats to your goat pen, the established ones will put the intruders in their place. Often one goat gets picked on by the others, and you'll end up having sympathy for that goat. Also, goats can tell you from other people and feel an attachment for you. People and goats can become very attached to each other. I don't know if I understand this type of attachment.

CHAPTER
• SIX •

BARTER

Bartering is much more than just a way to save money. It is an act of love that involves people doing things for each other. It is also a means of breaking away from the larger economy and thus insuring that the community will survive if or when the larger society collapses.

How Barter Works

To show how barter works, I'll zero in on a born trader—Glenda. Glenda loves to trade, even if she is only the middle person in a trade by others. She even has a large trunk in her car to carry things to trade. In it she keeps books, clothes, juice, eggs, and whatever else she happens to be trading. Her vehicle could be considered a combination book mobile, flea market, and grocery store.

Some of the trades Glenda is engaged in are direct, while others are like the rum-molasses-tea triangles we learned about in history class. Glenda trades babysitting for Jane's child, Amanda, for clothes that Jane sews for her. Sometimes Jane does grocery shopping for Glenda in return for babysitting. Glenda also trades with some people in town who prefer to drink the pure co-op water rather than the chlorinated town water. In return for gallon jars of water that Glenda gave Pam, Pam made draperies for Glenda.

A triangular trade emerges when someone can trade an item that can be traded for something else. Glenda gets a homemade fruit beverage from a friend in town which she trades to several people. The beverage is organic, has no preservatives, and has a fine taste, so it is in high demand. Glenda trades bottles of the drink for hair cuts with one person, for eggs and money with another, and for trips to the grocery store with still another. Often the drink is thrown in with other items in a swap, as when Glenda traded sausage, juice, and babysitting for a week's groceries.

All the exchanges described are outside the larger economy. The IRS doesn't know what to do about such instances. In fact, there is little that they can do. There are estimates that as much as twenty-five percent of the nation's business may be conducted through barter. In our case there is not much interest in avoiding taxes. The motivation is love. Someone has a surplus of one item, and they want to share it. Someone else has time but no money, so they do something in return for the item. People exchange on an equal basis.

Often people do things for others with no thought of a specific trade. Most people out here in our community believe that it is part of the natural order of things that a person should give and also take. This is the natural energy exchange that one has in working the land. You put something into the land, and you take something out. It would be unnatural to keep taking out without putting something back in. In our relations people often do things for others out of love, and their love is returned when the person they help has something to offer them. While we are not so calculating as to consciously compute such things, people do in fact build up credits by their acts of love.

When an individual has given an extraordinary amount of time to the community as a whole, as one person did in supervising construction work on our tractor shed, members of the community have come forth to offer to do work for that individual. They just go over to that person's house and ask him or her if there is anything they could help with. As anyone knows who has a friend or relative in the country, there are always plenty of chores that can be done.

A Barter Economy

Money has a different function in the barter economy than in the larger economy. It is used as a standard of value to determine how much of one thing should be traded for how much of something else. Money is not always regarded as something of value itself in the exchange. Money is often used only as a measure of value. Something else, such as hours of work, could be substituted as a measure of exchange, so a barter system is not dependent upon money.

If the economy collapses, or should I say when, people might want to switch to a labor exchange system. Perhaps our co-op by itself or with others could set up an inflation proof currency that is based on labor exchange with one unit of the currency being equal to one hour of labor.

Because money is used only to tell ratios between actual things for exchange purposes, a barter economy is inflation proof. If a dozen duck eggs are traded for a gallon of goats' milk because one dozen eggs cost $1.80, and a half-gallon of goats' milk costs $1.80, the ratio will not change if eggs and milk in the larger economy go up to $2.50. Exchange ratios are not affected by inflation. The issue in bartering is not so much one of bargaining as it is determining a fair exchange.

A barter economy has been known to help shield certain interdependent groups from the ravages of national depression. A community's well being depends on people's continuing to work to provide the goods people use. When a depression occurs, people don't work because, in the larger economy, people work for money. In the barter economy people still continue working because they are working for the things others, like themselves, are providing. In the larger economy people work only when the owners of industry can make a profit from their labor. In the barter economy people work for themselves. When times are hard in the larger economy, people in the barter economy still have work.

All you have to do to insure your economic well being is to pick something that you can produce easily and trade with others. For some on the co-op this is corn, for others goats' milk, another uses honey, and for still another it is his skill as a cabinet maker. Compared to the community route to a simple lifestyle, the individual route requires that each family either be an expert at producing everything or be dependent on the vagaries of the larger economy for those items they can't provide themselves.

Not everyone in the community engages in bartering or is concerned about becoming independent of the larger economy. To many people, an intentional community is simply a much better type of development, one in which there is a spirit of helping each other and getting to know your neighbors. But everyone knows that if the economy were to collapse, our community would be a very good place to be.

CHAPTER
• SEVEN •

INVESTING FOR PEOPLE WHO WANT TO RETIRE WHILE YOUNG

My wife and I finished building our home with money that had been going for rent, and when the house was comfortable, we started to apply that same item in our budget to an investment program. By living on a budget below our middle-class income, we were able to save $2,000 a year. After five years we had more than $10,000, and with wise investing $10,000 can provide you with an additional $2,000 a year. Your money's money starts to make money, and you become wealthier.

Planning Your Finances

You will have to put some energy into planning your finances—otherwise you won't realize the goal of financial independence. The goal of total financial freedom is attained only by long range planning. The one feature all of us in the land co-operative share is that we all have long range plans.

Not planning has disastrous effects. People with good incomes often find themselves destitute in their old age because they don't plan ahead. Only two out of a hundred people nationally are financially independent in their old age. Others have to work or are dependent on family, friends, or charity. To achieve financial independence you must have a plan, and this is especially true if you want to become financially independent while you are young and able to enjoy it.

Investment counselors have a saying that makes sense: "You don't get rich making money but by managing the money you make." You want to get the maximum from what you have, and to do this you must put your money into the right things. I've gone to several investment counselors to learn how to get the most from what I have. I warn you that I'm not an investment counselor and not an accountant, and I disclaim any responsibility for your spending all your money on what I advise. Having made that disclaimer, let me share with you what any competent investment counselor might tell you.

Put aside money regularly for investment purposes. Pay yourself first, before you pay your bills. Make saving for investment a regular habit. The suggestions in this book should help you live cheaply enough so that if you have an average income, you will end up with money to invest. Remember that the ability to save is not so much a factor of what you make but rather is the difference between what you make and what you spend. We don't have much control over what we can make, but most of us can adopt a simpler lifestyle that will allow us to save.

Investment counselors would tell you that there are two so-called investments that you should avoid. One is buying whole life or endowment insurance policies, and the other is putting money in the bank.

When insurance people sell whole life insurance policies, they claim that these policies are a means of savings because people get their money back after a period of time. What they don't tell people is that the buyers of this type of insurance sacrifice the interest on their money and end up paying many times the face value of their policies. As an investment, insurance stinks. You should view insurance as something for an emergency, and that's all. There is a type of life insurance that costs less than half what whole life costs for the same protection—it's called term life insurance—and that is the only kind I ever buy.

Many of my neighbors have no fire, health, or life insurance. They know that if someone's house is burnt down, the whole community would help build them another house. This might be true in my community, but my wife and I have fire insurance anyway. We'd never want to be a burden on any others, so we also have health and term life insurance.

Savings accounts are a terrible investment because the low rate of interest they pay doesn't even keep up with inflation. Another common so-called investment is annuity programs which allow people to save on taxes if they put money away for retirement. These have drawbacks because once again you get a low rate of return, and even worse, you can't get at your money (without paying a penalty) until you're too old to enjoy it. The question then becomes, "What is a good investment?"

Your First Investments

Your first investment should be, of course, a piece of land. That begins with buying land in a loving community. I really believe that this is the best investment you can make. Your second investment should be your home.

Investment people will usually tell you that it is best to borrow as much as you can because of what they call leverage, but I think that it's best to own your home with no mortgage. Here I diverge from what the counselors say because the needs of the person who is seeking the simple lifestyle differ from the needs of the person who is caught up in the rat race. Part of simplifying your life means you have the peace of mind of not ever worrying about having your home taken away from you.

Owning your home is better security for your old age than any annuity or pension could possibly be. There are towns filled with old people who have to scrounge around for a place to live. They live in retirement cities where the apartments they rent are turned into condominiums they cannot afford, and so they search continually for apartments. Many of these people have annuities and pensions which provide them with steady checks that become worth less and less as the cost of a place to live continues to rise. The only way to insure against worrying about a place to live is to own your home.

Third, you should invest in setting up your homestead so you can produce as much as possible yourself. This might mean buying good tools, investing in goats and chickens, or building up your compost heap. A good compost heap represents real wealth better than pieces of paper. After these investments have been made, you might want to try the more traditional ones.

The Traditional Investments

Investment counselors speak of cash equivalencies, liquid investments, and long-term investments. A cash equivalency fund is something like a bank account, or better yet, a money market account that pays interest at just below the current prime rate. Right now money market funds are paying fifteen percent, while the banks are paying five and a half. How much money you should have in a cash equivalency account depends on your lifestyle. If you're self-employed as an artist or craftsperson, then you should have at least a year's income available to tide you over a slow period so you don't have to take a regular job. If you're in a regular job, then you don't need to tie up much money in a cash equivalency—half a year's income is enough. You can make more money in other investments.

High liquidity investments might include owning silver, gold, stocks, certificates of deposit, government bonds, or investing in your own community. A community loan program that gives a higher rate of return than a bank account is described in Chapter Twelve. High liquidity investments do not allow you to get your money as quickly as with cash equivalencies, but they give you a higher rate of return. How quickly you can get your money depends on the investment. Silver and stocks are called highly liquid investments because you can sell them quickly. But don't be fooled—if the market price is below what you paid, then you won't find it easy to take a loss by selling.

The best long range investment is to buy single family homes, duplexes, and apartment buildings. People are able to get returns of thirty percent and more a year from investments in real estate. It is not unusual for someone to double money invested in one year.

Profits on rental properties are in large part due to the tax laws, which favor people who have money to invest, and due to inflation, which also benefits investors. To show how this works, I'll consider the benefits of buying a $45,000 home with a $5,000 down payment and a $40,000 mortgage at twelve percent. Interest payments of over $5,000 are deductible (along with taxes and maintenance), and would just about cancel income from rent. Meanwhile, an investor can claim depreciation of one-fifteenth of $45,000 or $3,000. If you pay a third of your income in taxes, this means you get to keep $1,000 more. In addition you get the appreciation of the house due to inflation. At a ten percent rate, this is an increase of $4,500 the first year, at fifteen percent, this is $6,750. The laws that allow an investor to depreciate a property while it is appreciating might appear unfair. Nevertheless, these laws exist, and you can take advantage of them. You don't abolish poverty by being poor.

It is very exciting to think of what will happen if you take the $2,000 or so you are now spending on rent or a mortgage, put that into building a house, and then put it into investments. Your $2,000 a year quickly becomes $10,000, and then $20,000, $40,000, and more. If you get thirty percent on your money, it will double about every three years. In thirty years you will have had ten doublings of your money. Even if you just used the first $10,000 and didn't add to it, you would have become a millionaire. That's what would happen if you reinvested all your profits. Of course, you'd have the sense to start spending your money long before that point.

COMMUNITY DYNAMICS

PART THREE

CHAPTER
• EIGHT •

STARTING A COMMUNITY

Y ou want to have a community of friends in the country, a community of people who like each other and are able to govern themselves in an amiable manner. At the present time you are living scattered about a city, living in less than the desired circumstances. How do you go from your present situation to the desired one?

It Begins with Meetings

You have to start with meetings at which you share your dreams and begin to forge new realities. Meetings may seem a drag, but they are necessary. Meetings aren't just a hurdle—they're an important part of forming a community. If someone could have a magic wand and have everyone immediately together in the country, they wouldn't be doing you any favor. A community formed without going through the process of meetings would fall apart. Through meetings people develop a pattern of working together. The more you iron out problems at the initial stages, the easier it is later on.

Deciding on the Type of Community You Want

There are as many different types of communities as there are motivations for changing one's life. The *Commune Directory* published by Communities Magazine lists survival groups, yoga retreats, religious, aesthetic, and environmental groups; collectives that publish books, grow food, and ones that run seminars, free schools, and health institutes. As diverse as these groups are, they display only a few different forms of land ownership. Land can be owned by one wealthy individual who allows people to settle at his or her pleasure. Land can also be owned by an organization, by the individuals in the community, or with a combination of private and community ownership.

Many communities are started by wealthy individuals with individual motives. One person may happen to own a large farm and want like-minded people as neighbors; another may own land and be unable to make payments without involving more people. A rich person may want to be a guru and may believe that forming a community is a way of securing followers. Someone else may want to live in the country and may prefer to do so in an intentional community.

One obvious problem with having a community on land that is owned by one individual, or one family, is that you end up with a class system in which the rest of the community can end up resenting the owners. The owners have all power over decisions because they own the land. If someone displeases the owners, they can force that person to leave. A community that exists on land owned by one individual cannot be a community of equals.

A second ownership scheme is to have land owned by an organization. Communities are sometimes organized around religious, political, or philosophical organizations. Individuals in these communities do not own the land they work, and when they leave the community they lose all claim to the land they helped improve. One exception is in the case of land corporations.

In a land corporation, the corporation owns the land, and individuals buy shares in the corporation. An individual receives the right to build a home on the land of the corporation. Of course he or she must try to find a spot that is not too close to other individuals' homes, and there has to be a mechanism to resolve difficulties regarding this. When a person wants to move on, they must sell their shares back to the corporation at the price the corporation decides.

The advantage of a land corporation is that it is a simple ownership structure. It does not require deeds, surveys, and the like. It appears ideal where there is a huge tract of wilderness that everyone wants to retain as wilderness. Problems can arise when people want to use a large tract of land for farming, or when individuals want to move and get back what they spent on their homes. Buying into a land corporation is at best risky for individuals who don't want to lose what they have.

A third ownership scheme is to have land owned entirely by individuals. This is what we usually have in the larger society. There is nothing communal about this, and individual land owners in cities, on farms, and sprawled out in suburbia have little of the feeling or benefits of community. The advantage of individual ownership is of course that a person can sell his or her land and receive a payment for money and energy put into improvements. The fault is that having entirely individual ownership precludes a sense of community.

A fourth ownership scheme allows for the development of community while also giving individuals the benefit of private ownership of land. Land co-operatives combine private ownership and community ownership of land. Each individual, or family, owns at least one private acre, and the entire community shares in the ownership of common land. The price of common land is included in the price of the individual acres, so when people sell their private acres they receive a price that includes both the private and communal lands.

Land co-ops, unlike communities owned by one wealthy individual, allow the possibility of creating a democratic communal government. Unlike communities that are owned by organizations, land co-ops do not require conformity to a set religious, political or philosophical viewpoint. In land co-ops individuals who may not be united in any other way can get together to buy land. If individuals decide to move, they can sell their land for whatever they can get: a feature that is not possible with land corporations. Land co-ops have all the advantages that come with individual ownership plus the features of community which are lacking in normal developments.

I'll describe land co-operatives the most because I think that this type of organizational structure is best, and also because I know the most about them. In a society where people move on the average of once every four years, I think that it is unrealistic to expect that no one will want to move. The land co-op structure has the advantage over other forms of communal ownership in that people can sell their land when they leave and get a return on their homes. Also, I like living in a community with a diversity of individuals. It simply wouldn't be as interesting to live among people who all think alike.

Land Co-operatives

My involvement in a land co-op started after attending a presentation. If you don't hear of one, get together with friends and plan your own. At the presentation those who are interested are asked to make some kind of commitment. A minimum commitment would be a $10 fee to receive mailings; a maximum would be several hundred dollars which would serve as a deposit on land.

The first problem is to get members for your community. At the organizational stage people pay to be on a waiting list to buy land in a community when neither land nor community exists. They will usually be reluctant to commit themselves; yet a commitment is necessary to get things started. A second problem will exist when the group actually buys the land and divides it. How will you decide who gets which piece of land? These two problems solve each other. The first to put their money down get first choice of land. Contracts are numbered, and people get priority in land choice according to the date they bought it. My number was seventeen, so if a conflict had arisen whereby a person with a higher number, say twenty-three, wanted the same piece of land that I wanted, then I would have had priority over that person. Conflicts are actually very rare because people differ tremendously in their tastes. I wanted half meadow and half climax forest. Others wanted all meadow, or all forest, or had special interests such as wanting to be next to a friend. Moreover, a high number does not doom a person to a poor selection because people come and go. Individuals with high numbers often ended up with land chosen by those who had first choice. Nevertheless, a policy of first-join, first-choice gives people an incentive to buy into the community quickly.

As soon as you have a group of people who have made a commitment to forming a community, you can establish the permanent committees which will follow you to the land. You might begin with a committee to start a newspaper. Add to this a committee to begin drafting a list of covenants and restrictions to apply to your land and a committee to look for possible locations. Others should be formed for making presentations, selling land, and financial planning. Still other committees might be formed for temporary activities such as having flea markets to raise money or advertising the land co-operative at a county fair.

Once you have a group of people who are seriously interested in buying land together, it is necessary to work out the covenants and restrictions which will apply to that land. Covenants and restrictions (C&R) are a legal document recorded in the courthouse along with the land deed you will eventually receive. It's important that people agree on the type of community they want to live in, and to some extent, the covenants and restrictions will define the type of community.

As the debate on covenants and restrictions gets under way, many people will decide that the community is not for them. This is natural, and it's best that the group sort itself out at this stage instead of after people have committed time and resources in building homes. Those who want to leave should be given their money back in full, except for the dues assessments which covered the newspapers they received, etc. To insure the survival of the group, it is desirable that twice as many people sign up as are thought necessary for buying land. Agreeing on covenants and restrictions is an attrition process. If not many quit, the group can form more than one co-op.

A model set of covenants and restrictions is included in Appendix I. It includes provisions to insure that areas of the common land will be kept in their natural state and that the minimum parcel of land that can be sold is one acre.

Most of the articles are not controversial. People interested in forming a land co-operative should be able to agree on such things as the need to prevent the wholesale cutting of trees. Some covenants, however, will bother people, such as the one allowing easements over or through individuals' land for the purpose of electric wires. Easements can be granted to the cooperative and not the electric company. That way the co-op can negotiate with the companies to insure that trees are not cut unnecessarily. Stating that the co-op has certain rights, or that certain things are forbidden, does not mean that the co-op will exercise its rights or that the forbidden actions cannot be allowed. The community still has the option of deciding what it wants to do and can even decide not to enforce certain restrictions. What the C&R does do is allow the co-op certain rights under law and protect it from being sued in court for certain actions. If you want to avoid legal hassles, it is best to put power in the hands of the co-op rather than the courts and then settle issues in the community.

But while most of the C&R articles are not even worthy of debate (they are just formalities), some will be hotly debated. People who own mobile homes may quit if restrictions are placed on mobile homes. People may argue over whether the co-op should have restrictions on the transfer of property—I recommend that there be no restrictions because restrictions tend to be unworkable. There may be fights over what activities should be prohibited. Some people may be opposed to hunting and the raising of animals for slaughter. We had lively debates on what type of commercial ventures should be allowed, with some individuals desiring a residential community and others wanting to earn their living on the land. In this process you will define the type of community you want yours to be, and people will decide whether they want to be members of the community.

Mistakes to Avoid

Don't start a co-op with one group of people with the idea that another group will take over at a later date. The transfer can get very complicated. The covenants and restrictions that you write should be intended as your final ones; and there should be no classes of people in your document. Our co-op started with two groups of people, the group that started the co-op and the membership of the community, and then had to go through a complicated process of switching rights and privileges from one group to the other. This transfer got very complicated because the group that started the co-op, M.L.I. (Misty Hills Land Incorporated), had committed themselves financially and legally and wanted to protect themselves by maintaining control of the co-op. Meanwhile a community had developed which consisted of people who desired self-government and wanted to liberate themselves from the originators, who were viewed as a separate group outside the community. If an organization such as Land Co-op Consultants (described in Appendix II) helps start the co-op, then there is no problem because they are outside the community. Problems arise when you have two classes of people within the community. Every attempt should be made to have one class of citizenship and to divide all responsibilities as equally as possible among those citizens. You want to set it up right the first time so that no transfer of power will be needed later on.

Another of our mistakes was making it too hard to change the covenants and restrictions. Inevitably some things will have to be changed, and they may be urgent. You don't want to put yourself in a position where you can't make needed changes because it is physically impossible to reach enough members. Our original covenants and restrictions stipulated that eighty-five percent of the members had to approve any change. Members were scattered before we moved to the land, and it was a Herculean task to gather signatures. A much more realistic figure is sixty percent.

Our community went through a very painful period because of these and other mistakes in our initial covenants and restrictions. For example, we made the mistake of not putting in clear easements for electrical wires. This mistake was made even worse by everyone's desire to come up with an ideal set of covenants and restrictions and their unwillingness to sign anything that wasn't perfect (in their eyes). A letter I wrote in the community newspaper will give you an idea of the mess we got ourselves into.

THE LEGAL FUND

"Let me see if I understand what people get when they join the co-op. They get their acre, plus a share of the common land, plus there is money for development. Is that right?"

"There once was a development fund, but we have a better use for it now. Remember, I explained how the co-op got started. This group decided to start a nonprofit development, a co-op. Well, one family in the co-op didn't like the way the electric easement went through their land, so they sued. Then the developers got frightened of being sued and decided on the advice of their lawyer to not grant any easements until the co-op members covered them legally by voting for a set of covenants and restrictions amendments. Various members, including myself, found faults with the different restrictions and refused to pass them. Meanwhile, some co-op members got a great idea. They decided to sue the developer for not granting easements. So the nonprofit development had suits against it for granting easements and for not granting easements.

"It's a great game. The co-op pays the legal fees, and any number can play. What we used to call "Development Fund" is now "The Legal Fund," and we all enjoy this so much that we're refusing to agree on a set of restrictions that would cover any more suits. Now another game is also being played. It's called "Set of Restrictions." We go through one set of restrictions after another. The council and M.L.I. each have their own set of restrictions. I don't like either and will be writing my own. This game is a lot more interesting than "Suing Over Easements." All one can do in that game is sue if an easement is granted and sue if an easement is not granted. In "Set of Restrictions" each member can formulate his or her own set of restrictions, and a whole bunch of people have to get eighty-five percent to vote on each different set."

In the end, though, it is better to have an imperfect set of covenants and restrictions than to have no set at all. If you have no clear set, then you can't enforce any of your rules, such as rules against cutting down all the trees on your land, and anyone can sue the co-op over anything. Nor will electric and phone companies run wires to your land unless easements are granted in C&R. Thus you should have a clear, enforceable set of covenants and restrictions at all times, even if the set fully suits no one. You need the protection of an enforceable set while you work on attaining agreement to a better one.

CHAPTER
• NINE •

COMMUNITY DECISION MAKING

There are several different ways a community might go about making decisions. Those that I describe here are majority rule, consensus, and what I call "professional planning." Majority rule means having at least fifty-one percent agree, consensus means having everyone agree, and professional planning involves using tools such as needs assessment questionnaires. We have used all three methods and continually argue over the merits and faults of each.

Majority Rule

Majority decision making is the method we Americans are most familiar with. It is the method used in our democratic institutions—the Congress, State Legislatures, and town councils. The method has been codified in Robert's Rules of Order. When we were in high school, we were told that Robert's Rules provide a guide to running meetings, and we followed those rules in our school student senates. When we use the word "democracy," we usually mean majority rule, not that other methods can't also be democratic. It can and will be argued later that consensual democracy is more democratic than majority democracy. But for now let's discuss what is usually meant by democracy.

Democracy requires that everyone abide by the decision of the majority. That means that some people may be unsatisfied with decisions and that the entire community does not have to worry about winning those people over. Indeed, it would be wrong for the community to spend time trying to win everyone over. Once a majority opinion is reached on a decision, the community should move on to other decisions.

There are some conditions that are necessary for democracy, and these conditions should be respected. Unanimity is not one of these conditions: people can be out-voted. Nonetheless, there are things that everyone, including those who are out-voted, is entitled to. Everyone is entitled to an opportunity to pursuade others. Everyone is entitled to an opportunity to contact their representatives on issues before the representatives vote, and everyone is entitled to access to all the facts that can be made available which are relevant to decisions. Everyone is also entitled to the opportunity to know the decision alternatives, and the arguments for each alternative.

All members of the community are entitled to the above conditions, which I believe are necessary for democracy to be meaningful. In the land co-op situation, insuring these conditions amounts to the following:

1. The business of town council meetings should be announced and posted in advance so that members can give their representatives feedback.

2. Facts which are necessary for intelligent decision making should be provided to the membership in our community media, which is our newspaper, the Alternate Current. The paper should include articles outlining alternate actions and arguments for each.

3. A forum should be provided, either in the media or by means of public meetings, for an exchange of views on issues. Those advocating each view should take the time to prepare defenses for their positions.

At one of our meetings a member complained that she did not know what had been going on with regard to a particular issue. One person responded to her complaint by saying, "Well, you'd know if you went to the meetings of the financial planning committee, the 2001 Committee, and the town council meetings." This may be true, but it is unfair. Everyone cannot be expected to go to all meetings—in fact, it is physically impossible for everyone to go to all committee meetings. But everyone does have a right to access to information. The proper source for information is in the community media that everyone has access to.

Communication is crucial to the working of democracy. Meaningful decisions are informed decisions. Freedom of choice is meaningless if people cannot know their choices, present new choices, and have an opportunity to win others to their side.

After forming committees, which is of course necessary, there is a problem of keeping people informed of what the committees are doing. When an organization functions, it can develop a gap whereby committee members have knowledge that the remainder of the group lacks. This can result in committee members being ahead of the community on an issue. The committee members then feel that the rest of the group is holding them back, and they may want to be given decision powers so that the others cannot slow them down. The better solution is for the committee members to use available means to inform the rest of the community. It is not healthy for one group in the community to be working with one set of facts, while other groups work with other facts. People may end up disagreeing on values and attitudes, but they can at least reach agreement on their facts by communicating with each other.

Democracy can work, and its ways are really very simple. People should be informed that a decision is to be made, should be given access to the relevant facts, and be given an opportunity to hear various sides of issues. And then everyone should abide by the decision of the majority. If people are out-voted after being given a chance to win others over to their view, then they have no right to stop the proceedings of the entire community. If the minority feels that their views were not given a fair chance, that the necessary conditions listed above were not present, then it might be justified to have a second vote to provide time to discuss an issue. To insure the avoidance of any claims of unfair treatment, it may be desirable to have a policy of voting on important issues twice with the second vote being the final one. The purpose of the second vote would be to insure that there is time for people to consider issues. It is not a means by which an out-voted minority can paralyze the body politic.

Consensual Decision Making

To understand consensus decision making, it is helpful to first understand the limits of majority decision making. Majority decision making limits meetings to a debate format and precludes more creative problem solving. If you follow Robert's Rules of Order, one person makes a motion, and then people speak either for or against the motion, and a vote is taken. New solutions are not easily introduced. You either accept the motion on the floor or you reject it. People are forced to take sides. When a vote is taken, someone wins and someone loses. It is the last feature of majority rule that makes majority rule undesirable for a community. With consensual decision making, every attempt is made to come up with decisions that everyone can live with.

Consensual decision making aims at having a situation in which everybody wins. Instead of having individuals making motions which are accepted or rejected, everyone is invited to suggest ideas which then belong to the group. The model for consensual decision making is a problem solving model. Everyone works together at defining a problem, thinking of alternative solutions, and choosing a course of action.

The key to successful consensual decision making is to have good meeting facilitators. One of the facilitator's roles is to protect individuals from attack and to encourage people to participate. Another role is to focus the group on common tasks. A technique that is effective in keeping the group on task is to use a problem solving model that breaks the problem down into discreet tasks, such as defining the problem, listing alternative solutions, and judging between solutions. The facilitator should see to it that people do not start judging ideas when the group is at the stage of listing possibilities. People should be able to suggest ideas without having their suggestions criticized. Later, when the ideas have been listed and belong to the group rather than individuals, the ideas can be judged.

Another function that should be performed with consensual decision making is the recording of suggestions that are made at meetings. This can be done by using a large newsprint pad. The advantage of recording comments is that people can be assured that their ideas are being considered, and people are less likely to repeat the same ideas when the ideas are already written down in front of them. The names of the originators of the ideas are, of course, omitted, so that there is less ego involvement. Once ideas are listed, they are the property of the community.

When a consensus has been reached, it should be recorded. One problem that sometimes exists with consensual decision making is that it is sometimes hard to know when a decision has been made. We have had occasions when someone has said "But I thought we had reached a decision on that" when most people did not believe they had agreed to anything. This problem doesn't exist with majority decision making because decisions are made when votes are tallied. One approach to solving this problem would be for the facilitator to ask, "Have we reached a consensus on this issue?" and to then have the recorder note that a decision has been made. Another solution would be to take votes, but that doesn't seem consistent with consensus.

Professional Planning

Majority rule and consensus both assume that people know what is best for them. Professional planning assumes that planners can sometimes know better than individuals what is best for the individuals. We have had some evidence that supports the professional approach to planning.

In order to make decisions intelligently on how we might spend our development funds, we asked people what they wanted to spend the money on, and we also conducted a needs assessment. The results show the difference between a list of what people want and what they need and also show the importance of doing a needs assessment.

In listing what they wanted, almost everybody in the co-op included "a community center" at the top of their list, along with a swimming place and other things. The list of wants simply asked people to list what they thought we should spend the money on.

A needs assessment is a more complex instrument. It asked such things as "How much time would you spend at a community center?" with a choice between 0, 1, 2, 3, or more hours a week. It also asked detailed questions such as:

"Which rooms would you use most?"

"If we had a communal kitchen, how many meals a week would you be interested in having at the community center?"

The needs assessment was geared not just to determine whether people needed a community center but to determine what rooms people would use. While many people listed that they wanted a large kitchen, few people indicated that they would use such a facility. People also listed that they wanted a large meeting room, but once again few people indicated that they would use such a room.

The importance of doing a needs assessment, asking people what they would actually use, is that it prevents a situation of building something that everyone says they want but no one will ever use. The difference between needs and wants was startling as we began our planning.

We use questionnaires as an information device rather than as a decision making device. After learning that few people would actually use a large kitchen in a community center, people started to change their minds about wanting such a facility. Rather than having an elite of professional planners who tell the group what to do, we use professional planning tools for information and keep power in the hands of the individuals who are affected by decisions.

Some people in our community have been frustrated by this and would prefer that the community be governed by a professional board. They reason that most people are not concerned about most of the decisions and that professionals can know what people want by using questionnaires.

I think that a desirable approach to the democracy vs. professional planning controversy is to have the ultimate power rest in democratic decision making and to use professional planning methods for gathering information. This means that individuals should have the sense to use the results of professional level studies in their voting. It also means that people should allow leaders of their own choosing enough power so that they can do a decent job. Democracy does not mean that everyone has to make every single decision but that ultimate power for decision making rests with the citizens of the community.

CHAPTER
• TEN •

GETTING THINGS DONE

S tarting a community involves a lot of work, so you might as
well understand how people get things done. You're going to
have to find out who in your group likes to talk and who likes to
get things accomplished. You're also going to have to learn how
to run meetings. You can waste an awful lot of time at meetings
if you don't avoid certain pitfalls.

Pitfalls to Avoid

One pitfall to avoid is the belief that committees get things done.
Someone at a meeting will suggest the formation of several committees, each of which is to meet and interact with the others. One
committee will be proposed to design a community center, another to
handle the financing of the center, and still another committee to
co-ordinate the first two committees. What such grandiose suggestions
forget is that no matter what committees you have, the work will still
be done by individuals. It's better to assign a task to an individual than
to a nonexistent committee.

A second pitfall to avoid is the attempt to work out plans in
abstract form. Agreement in the abstract means nothing because each
person may picture what you're agreeing on differently. We went about
planning the use of our common land in the abstract for several years
and got nowhere. Then one member, Roger, put a plan on paper.
Once we had a real plan to criticize, people could either accept it or
change it. The discussion all of a sudden became fruitful.

Still another pitfall to avoid is the attempt to conduct
philosophical discussions at business meetings. The two don't mix.
There isn't enough time at business meetings for people to convince
each other of philosophical viewpoints. Such discussions just go on

and on without closure. At a business meeting the amount of time spent discussing each issue should be limited in advance.

Separate meetings should be held for discussing broad issues. To this end we set up a discussion group, the 2001 Committee, which was open to all members and devoted to discussing the direction of our co-operative. People were able to share their visions at this meeting, and there was time for people to try to win others over, something that never seemed to happen at business meetings.

There is a tendency for the community to dump every crisis on the broad issue discussion groups, so that they don't get a chance to discuss the larger issues. Our committee that was discussing issues of how we want to govern ourselves got stuck with the problem of hiring a new co-ordinator, and our committee that was considering the long range direction of the community got bogged down for awhile in architectural drawings of a community center. You should try to keep the day-to-day issues out of the meetings at which you discuss broad issues, or you won't ever get beyond the daily crisis.

While business and general philosophy discussions should be kept separate, there is an interaction between the two. If people share general beliefs about the direction of the community, it will be easier to make everyday decisions. Energy and time should be devoted to developing common beliefs and a feeling of community. It is valuable to have open ended discussions but not at the business meetings. It is also valuable to just hold hands and chant a mantra together. Anything that you do that helps people to know and understand each other, and feel good vibrations together, will help the community in all its endeavors.

How to Run Meetings

Meetings, meetings, meetings—you're going to have a lot of meetings, so you may as well learn how to run them. There are several factors which can determine whether your meetings are productive or a waste of time. This list is compiled from experience, from trial and error, mostly from error. After listing the things you should do to insure productive meetings, I list some of the wrong things we have done. As you will see, the role of the moderator of a meeting is crucial for avoiding wasted meetings.

First, a meeting should be scheduled for a realistic hour that will allow the time necessary for the business of the meeting. Once an important meeting was scheduled for 11 a.m. on a Sunday. We quickly went into lunch time, and people started to go home for lunch. Any meeting should be scheduled so that it can go for the length of time necessary.

Second, meetings should begin at the time they are scheduled to begin. We have had moderators who just stood around talking when meetings were supposed to begin. Often members have had to ask moderators to call meetings to order. Whoever is assigned as a moderator should call the meeting to order on time.

Third, there should be an agenda for the meeting in advance so that everyone can know what will be discussed. Sometimes our moderators have done this, and sometimes they have not. When they do not, there is often confusion over what the meeting is about. At times it has appeared that meetings were being held just for the sake of holding meetings.

Fourth, the charge of the meeting should be clearly understood. We have been faced with the situation of no one knowing which group in the co-op had the ability to make certain decisions. This happened when we considered the purchase of additional land. It wasn't clear whether the entire membership was needed for a decision or whether a decision could be made by the town council. When a general membership meeting was called, no one knew whether those at the meeting had the power to make a decision.

Fifth, a moderator should insure that people focus on the issue that is before the body. We have had instances where motions have been made and seconded and never voted on. At one meeting a motion was made that stated that since attendance at the meeting was low, no vote should be taken at the meeting. No vote was taken on this motion despite the fact that it was seconded. Instead, a discussion of the merits of the issue at hand took place, followed by voting on the issue. In the end the group could not decide whether the vote should count because of the low attendance—an issue that would have been settled if the group had voted on the original motion.

Sixth, a moderator should help facilitate a decision. Sometimes our moderators have been content to encourage far ranging discussion rather than helping to focus discussion. Once when people were discussing whether a particular price for land was fair, our moderator added to the discussion by saying "And of course there is also the issue of our setting priorities for all the other things we want." Then the moderator entertained a far ranging discussion of all the other things we might want and the problem of setting priorities. What would have been a discussion of one issue—whether the price of land was a good one for the co-op—became a discussion of several complex issues. The moderator let people add new issues and added to theirs. A moderator should help people come to a decision, not encourage people to talk. There is a difference between being the moderator of a T.V. discussion show and the moderator of a business meeting. The moderator of a business meeting should try to get the group to move toward a decision.

The Standard Code of Cooperative Procedure

To prevent some of the problems mentioned above, one of our members formulated a list of procedures which we now follow at our town council meetings with some success. These rules were formulated by David Joseph Brightbill.

RULE 1—RIGHT TO SPEAK

One person, and only one person, has the right to speak at any one time during meetings.

RULE 2—RECOGNITION

If a person wishes to speak, s/he shall non-verbally indicate the desire in some manner to the moderator.

RULE 3—MODERATOR

The moderator shall enforce these rules, arrange the agenda, recognize members to speak, and arbitrate disputes between members of the Council. The moderator shall refrain from participation in discussions. If need be, the moderator may appoint someone as temporary moderator for a given issue.

RULE 4—SCOPE OF DISCUSSION

One and only one proposal may be discussed at any one time, and no other business shall be conducted until that proposal is either decided upon, or postponed until a later time.

RULE 5—ORDER OF BUSINESS

The order of business at meetings shall be: (1) Call to order by the moderator, (2) Brief report on the last meeting, (3) Reports of any special crews, committees, etc., (4) Old and pending business, (5) New business, (6) Announcements, etc., (7) Announcement of next meeting time and place, and adjournment.

RULE 6—VOTING

A decision on each issue in the form of a motion shall be

determined by a majority vote. A motion may be called to a vote by a request to vote immediately, either by a member or by the moderator. If there is any objection, a two-thirds vote of the members present is necessary to vote immediately.

RULE 7—AGENDA

For an item to be considered for placement on the agenda at a meeting, that item shall be written on one side of one 9½ × 4¾ inch card, and given to the moderator before the meeting starts. All agenda cards shall be signed by the person submitting the item. Only business on the agenda shall be considered.

RULE 8—RECORDS

After an item has been disposed of, the moderator shall note the disposition and date on the back of the card. These cards shall constitute the record of business and shall be kept available in the Community Center to all interested persons.

Any items left pending shall be kept separate and shall be placed on the agenda when appropriate.

At the start of each Council meeting, a card shall be signed by each Council member, noting the group represented. These cards shall be used to divide the card file into sections representing each meeting.

RULE 9—QUORUM

No business shall be conducted by the Council without a majority of the entire present.

RULE 10—AMENDMENT TO THE RULES

These rules may be amended by a two-thirds vote.

Since the adoption of these procedures provides for writing proposals and action taken on proposals on cards during the meetings, these cards will be used as a source of accurate information concerning meeting decisions.

Getting People to Work

Once decisions have been made, they must be implemented. Some people thought that because we are a cooperative, people should line up to volunteer for tasks. What has actually happened is that we have a few people who volunteer, and these people sometimes resent the members who do not volunteer. One member who volunteered to work on a volunteer fire department benefit wrote this in our community paper.

THOUGHTS ON RECRUITING RELUCTANT
VOLUNTEERS

Another event is over. Everyone attending had a fine time, the eating was delectable, the cleanup reasonable, the meeting attendance rather poor considering the public officials we had on hand. And I think back over my frustrations of the last weeks. Mainly the lack of help I got, after repeated posted requests, with the leafleting effort in the VFD response area. With hindsight, one might say it didn't do any good—no one seemed to respond to it.

A very common phenomenon in many organizations is volunteer burnout. A few people volunteer because they think everyone ought to volunteer. When others do not volunteer, the few volunteers are stuck with the task. After a while, the pool of volunteers gets reduced, so more and more work is done by fewer and fewer people. Then a gap sets in between those doing the work and those who benefit and do nothing.

Alternatives to a purely voluntary system include requiring everyone to work a set number of hours a week and paying people. Many co-ops, such as food co-ops and book co-ops, require people to put in a small number of hours, or they give discounts to those who do. I think that a system that allows people a discount on their assessment fees for hours worked is desirable. The other alternative, paying people, has advantages and disadvantages. The advantage is that it can insure that jobs get done. The disadvantage is that once you turn a volunteer task into a paid job, people tend to stop volunteering. Also, in an egalitarian community, you don't want to divide between employees and employers.

Prisoners of Our Own Dogma

I don't have any easy solution to the problem of getting people to work. It's important to be open-minded to what will and will not work. I think that in my community we are often prisoners of our own dogma—we've tended to stick to policies long past the point where we could see that they do not work. One of our dogmas has been to over-rely on volunteerism. Another of our dogmas has been to avoid requiring people to do anything because we felt that such requirements would be coercive. In situations where everyone benefits equally—as in labor unions, fire protection, and co-operatives—it is sometimes necessary to use coercion to insure that people contribute equally; otherwise you have free riders. In the example of raising money for a volunteer fire department, it would be possible to levy a small tax on everyone in the protected area. Were that done it would not be necessary to plead for volunteers to go door to door. But, alas, it would be using coercion.

Another of our dogmas is our feeling that because we are a co-op, we must do everything co-operatively. Some people believe that everyone must do everything as group. There are people in our community who want to have more farm land. They could get together and buy more land as a small group. Instead they continually try to convince the entire community of the need for more land. For the entire co-op to buy land requires the approval of everybody and makes the task very difficult. Those who want land would be better off getting together and buying land on their own.

The feeling that everyone has to do everything together—that everybody must do this, or everybody must do that—prevents people from getting things done. If an activity is going to affect everyone, then you do require the group's approval; but if an activity, such as farming, can be successful without the entire group, then it is foolish to try to involve the entire group. The advantage of living in a land co-operative is not that the co-op as an organization will do things but that the people in the community are freer to do things.

There are ways the co-op can help individuals to realize their dreams. I include some of these in Chapter Fifteen. We must not forget that individuals have individual dreams. If we limit what people can do to what an organization can agree on, then individuals are stifled. The function of the community should be to support the individuals in it. What we must not forget is that it is individuals who get things done.

CHAPTER ·ELEVEN·

BUILDING A SENSE OF COMMUNITY

A s great as the material benefits of living in a land co-operative are, the spiritual benefits are far greater. I have gotten some of the greatest highs in my life from the people in my community. How can you put a price on the joy of an old fashioned community Thanksgiving feast shared with a hundred people, a neighborhood festival of volleyball and music, of people dancing around a campfire, or people sharing their common concerns and problems in a circle of friendship? I only know that my life would be a lot less rich without these experiences.

Spiritual Benefits of a Community

From time to time people have shared statements of what a community means, statements that they've written as well as they have read. I'll share a couple of these with you.

From the St. Johnsbury, Vermont, Town Plan:

There is a need for intimate human relationships, for the security of settled home and associations, for spiritual unity, and for orderly transmission of the basic cultural inheritance. These the small community at its best can supply. Whoever keeps the small community alive and at its best during this dark period, whoever clarifies, refines, and strengthens the vision of the small community, may have more to do with the final emergence of a great society than those who dominate big industry and big government.

And from Abbe Sieyes, France, 1789:

If only men would see each other as the agents of each other's happiness, they would occupy the earth, their common habitation, in peace, and move forward confidently to their common good.

Respect for Community Property

I have witnessed the evolution of our separate households into a community and the development of devotion to the community. This is symbolized for me in the way people in the co-op take care of community property. Our first community property was a common mailbox—our first reaction was to let the mailbox rot away. We let our community property rot, just as people throughout the United States let their community property—the schools, the parks, and the cities—rot. At one point the mailbox was so eaten by termites that it wavered on three legs and stood waiting to fall on those who dared to get their mail.

Many have decried the decline of the commons in the western world. During the middle ages people were able to share land without spoiling what they shared. Individuals were granted the right to graze their animals on common land, and they did not overgraze the land. Now, businesses dump wastes in our commonly owned waterways. They strip forests, and in general private entrepreneurs show no regard for things that are owned in common. Individuals act for themselves and show no regard for others or things that are shared with others.

We started with the values of the wider society, with its disregard for community, and ended up respecting the rights of others and caring for our communal property. Our method involved building a loving community through celebrations and work. I do not know which of our activities contributed most to the change in attitude toward communal property, but I do know that a change occurred. People now feel a love of community which is reflected in the fact that people come forth to do work for the community, and people now take care of our common possessions.

Community Celebrations

There are many things that you can do to foster a sense of community. For one thing, you can have festivals and celebrate holidays together. We celebrate Thanksgiving, Christmas, Easter, Passover, and a few holidays of our own such as New Moon Festival. Our community is composed of people of all backgrounds and we share our celebrations—to the point that our children's religion may be a new one.

You can get an idea of one of our celebrations from this invitation that appeared in our community newspaper. Ours is a small community, and it is not unwieldy to post a notice inviting everyone to an individual's home.

Thanksgiving

November 27, 1975, is a day to circle in red on your calendar to remind you not to miss the Second Annual Thanksgiving Day Celebration on the Land. Festivities are to commence early in the afternoon in the vicinity of the domes, and dinner is to be eaten about 3 or 4 (perhaps both).

FOOD

Each group will prepare enough food to feed itself and its guests and should coordinate its efforts to assure a variety of dishes and drinks. Also, a card should be prepared for each dish showing ingredients (possibly even the recipe) and identifying the creator. All food will then be shared by members and their guests, as at last year's dinner.

ACTIVITIES

Plans now include volleyball, ping-pong, horseshoes, and music, possibly dancing, and a fire. If you have other ideas, bring them with you. (A TV will even be available nearby for those incorrigible football freaks.)

WORK PARTIES

There will be a brief work party at the domes on Saturday morning, November 22, to help prepare the site, and another Friday, November 28, to repair the site. No one who wishes to attend will be turned away!

TOOLS

Each member and each guest should bring and take away again a plate, bowl, cup, fork, spoon, knife, and anything else he or she may need to get through the meal in a somewhat civilized manner.

EXCUSES

There will be no excuses for missing the Second Annual Thanksgiving Day Celebration!!

This note appeared a couple of weeks after a Thanksgiving celebration:

It was delightful having Thanksgiving with 150 to 175 people.

The following items were left at our house after the Thanksgiving feast by people attending:

Mini-wheelie (child's riding toy)
crock with lid
pink towel monogrammed "MEK"

2 receiving blankets
2 carving knives
1 paring knife
2 pie tins
7 glass dinner plates
1 white corning pyroceram butter dish
2 platters (one white and one pink)
6 forks
6 serving & teaspoons (2 silver plate)

We'd like to see these get back to their owners . . . However, they have been around so long they almost seem like ours.

Marlene

Christmas

Our community reaches out beyond the physical borders of the land co-operative. A farmer who lives near the co-op invited people to his home to help decorate a Christmas tree. This is how the event was recorded in our paper.

SHINE ON—Symbolizing Community

Kate and Ed have done it again. By planning an activity which brought us all together—working and playing. Community demonstration at its best. The activity? Decorating their Columbian spruce. Over forty persons decorated, drank, ate, and played touch football. A new tradition has been established. Thanx to Kate and Ed.

As you drive by the tree all aglow some evening, think community. Putting it all together is what we're all about.

Gerry

Easter and Passover

Between Christmas and Easter there is usually a lull in activity, which is broken by a flurry of events in April. A special invitation is extended to the Good Friday Supper:

AN INVITATION TO GOOD FRIDAY SUPPER—

Once again I would like to extend an invitation to all members of our community to join a soup supper on Good Friday evening from 6 to 8 p.m. This meal has become a very symbolic, meaningful gesture for me—an opportunity to provide for and nourish some of those I hold most dear as our Mother Earth nourishes and provides for all of us. It seems I look forward to this gathering with more pleasure each year! Please join us on Friday between 6 & 8 p.m. and bring a bowl.

94

We start our celebration of Easter by doing yoga chants until the sun rises—our Easter sunrise service. Then we visit the gardens of all who invite us and share breakfast at a couple of homes. Within a week or two of Easter, people also participate in a Passover-Seder in the woods, sometimes followed by international folk dancing around a campfire. Everyone is proud of their heritage, and this pride is shared by all in the community.

A Holiday of Our Own

We have one holiday of our own—the New Moon Festival which occurs in early May. In addition to the customary May Pole, we have music and a bake sale. This is what one of our advertisements looked like.

NEW MOON FESTIVAL
SHARING & PERFORMANCE COMMITTEE SAYS:
"GONNA BE A REEELY BIG SHOW!"

We are aiming at a schedule like this:
Music
Speeches from invited guests
Variety
Music
LAND CO-OP SPEAKERS & PERFORMERS
Music

Invited speakers include people to speak in these areas: native American contributions, political perspectives, spiritual directions, local history and more.

The "variety" section includes invitations to dancers, humorists, poets and actors.

The invited musicians range from gospel to folk to jazz to semi-classical and a banjo picker.

BUT THE BEST PART WILL BE YOU, US, ALL. We've allotted an hour, but it can be more, for five minute speeches, performances, sharings, whatever and however FROM US TO OUR-SELVES.

We hope many co-opers will want to take this opportunity to share their thoughts.

Marriages on the Land

Gatherings are easier in our community where there is a tradition of pitching in and sharing at pot luck buffets. At our neighborhood meetings everyone brings a covered dish. A large affair, such as a wedding, is not much more complex than a buffet. It's certainly nothing to spend thousands of dollars on. Some of the most beautiful ceremonies are the simplest and easiest to arrange.

MARRIAGE ON-THE-LAND
COME ONE! COME ALL!
All Co-op members and all friends of the Co-op are invited to the wedding of George and Susan on their land at 4:00 p.m., October 15th. The ceremony will be both non-traditional and very informal. A campfire supper is planned for the entire evening. Beverages and unlimited quantities of vegetable stew will be available, but since it is impossible to plan more precisely with such an open invitation, your contribution to the buffet table will be welcome.

Parties

And of course there are parties. We love parties and are willing to share them. Often people share birthday parties by throwing a party for all those born under a certain astrological sign, such as a Pisces party. Both children and adults are the center of attention at these celebrations.

People are free to have private parties also. Everyone respects other people's right to privacy. The co-op is a great place to entertain people. It's something of a treat for people to be invited out here. Often we entertain on our deck or by the campfire site so that there is no problem in cleaning up.

After completing our forty by eighty foot community center we started having larger parties—parties that many in our community felt were getting too large. At some of our parties there were more people from off the land than on. We started getting people from the city who came out late and got drunk and obnoxious. Now we limit our gatherings to community members and their guests, and community members are responsible for their guests.

We have parties to raise funds for things like our volunteer fire department, and we have parties for the sake of having parties. Even people who aren't usually into parties enjoy our parties. Laurie wrote,

Three years ago I stood among the wallflowers—watching the crowd—lost in thought. Suddenly Gerry pulled me into the moving masses. Coaxed out of my inhibitions and into the arena of frenzied community, I have been dancing ever since. I've gone other places to dance; my feet don't move the same, my mouth doesn't ache from smiling, my clothes stink of smoke, and I've got to drive home when I'm through. However, none of these phenomena compare to the

96

missing appreciation of our community. When we're dancing and talking and scheming and smiling—children sleeping in the kitchen— the oft-missed bliss of pure joy returns. We're onto something special!

Moving
TO YOUR LAND

CHAPTER · TWELVE ·

BUYING YOUR LAND

I f things are going satisfactorily, you should still have a large group of people who want to live together in the country. You have been meeting regularly to work out covenants and restrictions, and in this process you have become a community. Your community newspaper has been reaching out to people, even to the people who were unable or unwilling to attend meetings. Committees have been working at putting the paper out, at running flea markets, at preparing meetings, and at looking for land. You've got a few possibilities you like and think you might be ready to move your community. At this point, if not before, you'd better have a tight organization. The work involved in purchasing land and beginning the move is going to require a co-ordinator, preferably full-time but at least part-time, in addition to a part-time accountant, who will be aided by your financial planning committee.

Getting Ready

If you want to keep your costs down, it will be best for you to do as much as you can by volunteer labor. You'll still need at least one person working regularly as co-ordinator, and it's only fair to pay this person. You might want help from Land Co-op Consultants for a brief period to get things going. After reading this book you'll know quite a bit about starting a community, but will still lack the experience of having gone through the process. Anyone who has helped start a co-op could provide an added impetus and testimony that it both can be done and is worth the effort.

When we started, we underestimated the job of organizing a land co-operative, and one individual, Jeff, thought that he could do the job on a part-time, unpaid basis. But Jeff soon found that he was faced with a choice of having the work interfere with his making a living or letting the work go. He noted in our community newspaper,

> In my case, I actually thought that my full-time services would not be needed. For almost four months I worked for free, thinking that any time now I could get back to earning my living in real estate. Deeply in debt after that period, I began charging a token amount and took on two major real estate projects to provide living money. But this caused development to greatly decelerate as we depended on volunteer efforts by people completely inexperienced in most real estate development matters; as a result of this, and of my lack of time and other factors, great personal friction resulted.

Below is an ad that appeared in our paper for a land co-op co-ordinator.

CO-OP COORDINATOR WANTED

> New position for coordinator of land cooperative is open to begin January 1, 1975, or sooner; hours and salary negotiable. Duties include general office work, coordination of all volunteer and business activity, handle general membership problems, and maintain positive communication with such groups as the electric company and city and county agencies. Applicants should prepare a written resume which should also include your concept of the position, how you intend to handle the position and why you wish to hold the position.

Once the co-op has purchased land and the community is more settled, the nature of the co-ordinator's job will change. At that point you will not need a dynamic leader who can motivate volunteers as much as you will need a business manager. Once you are set up, you will need someone who can carry out such mundane functions as making sure taxes are paid and insurance is taken care of, checking the monthly financial reports, and seeing to it that payments are made by everyone each month.

Selecting Land

You have many advantages because you are buying a large tract of land with a group. The price you will pay per acre is much lower than you would normally pay. In our case an acre of land was selling for $3,300 in 1973, but we were able to buy 240 acres at $1,333.33 an acre. Also, because you are going to have areas of natural preserve which you will hold in common, it is not necessary that every acre be habitable. You do need enough land that is dry enough or flat enough so that everyone can build a home on his or her individual acre, but wet or mountainous common lands are desirable for wildlife. Still another advantage is that you may be able to strike up a deal in the purchase of your land. People who sell large tracts usually don't want a large sum of money at once because of taxes. They are better off if the money comes in smaller amounts over a period of years. This will make it easier for you to arrange financing.

Figuring the Sales Price of an Acre

In figuring the sale price of an acre of land in your co-operative, you should keep in mind that the sale price must include money for both the common land held together and development funds. We were able to get 240 acres of land for $1,333.33 an acre. Since we planned to have 80 acres of this land as common land, the sale price for the remaining 160 acres would have to cover the cost of the full 240. Also added onto the cost of the land was money for development ($108,000) and contingencies ($10,000). The two last items were underestimated, and I'd advise a higher proportion. Even with some of the cost going for common land and development, buying land in a land co-op is not more expensive than buying individual acres on your own. This is because land bought in large tracts costs less than half what individual acres cost. So you can get the benefit of buying land in a co-op for no more than you would pay buying land by yourself.

We charged twice as much for two acres as for one, even though a person buying two acres would get no more use from the common land and development than a person buying one acre. Your group might want to charge less for multiple acres. This would encourage people to buy more than one acre, which is desirable for the community as a whole as it lessens the density.

The Down Payment

Our total land cost $320,000, of which $45,600 cash was required as a down payment. Before buying the land, we lined up $98,100 to include, in addition to the down payment, $52,500 for cash on hand. You have to have a large amount of cash on hand to cover mortgage payments, or you'll be in danger of losing your down payment. You might figure that it is necessary to have one-fourth to one-third of the money necessary for the purchase of your land lined up before you begin.

Where does the money come from? There are several sources. First there are the deposits people make when they put their names on the waiting list. This, together with additional money collected right before you purchase land, constitutes the down payment. You might want to charge from one-tenth to one-fourth the price of land as down payment, depending on what you can arrange. If you charge the smaller amount, however, you are going to need more money than you can raise from just the down payments. You might want to keep the down payments small in order not to exclude people of limited financial ability. To make up the difference, you could set up a community loan program, which is discussed below.

Starting a Community Loan Program

A co-op loan program gives investors interest on the money they loan, secured by a mortgage on the land. You might have loans from people both in and outside your community. These loans should be designed to be a reasonable investment for those who make them. Basically they work like a certificate of deposit, which requires some warning for withdrawal and pays a higher rate of interest than one can get in a regular bank account. When investors requested their money and we had the cash to spare, we simply returned their money. If we didn't have the cash on hand, we asked people to make extra payments on their land, or pay off their land entirely, so that we could return the investor's money. We never charged any penalty for early withdrawal and always paid a much higher return than the bank pays. At the worst, investors had to wait a few months to get their money. People who loan money to the co-op should understand that the co-op requires some warning before withdrawal.

The Project Financial Summary

As soon as you have a piece of land in mind that you are serious about, you should work out a financial summary. This is necessary so you can analyze the feasibility of purchasing the land, and it will also be necessary when you go to the bank for loans. The first part of the financial summary would list land, development, and contingency costs, and other parts would break these factors down more completely, such as dividing the land cost into the various individual mortgages and down payments. Below is a simplified version of the financial summary of the M.L.C.

Project Totals

Land cost (240 acres) $320,000
Development 108,000
Contingency .... _10,000_
   TOTAL $438,000

Co-signers for a Bank Loan

Unless the seller is financing the land, you are going to have to get a loan from a bank for the bulk of your land purchase. The question arises, "Who is the bank loaning the money to?" Banks prefer to deal with individuals rather than organizations, especially organizations that have no assets. To get a loan it will probably be necessary to line up members of your community who have assets and are willing to co-sign the note together. These individuals will be risking their assets on the success of the co-op and will have every incentive to make sure that the co-op follows responsible financial policies.

Someday, I hope there will be an organization that can insure loans to land co-ops and charge a fee for pledging assets. Land co-ops might want to include in their covenants and restrictions that a proportion of their development money should go to help form other co-ops. It would be a great stimulus to the development of co-ops if it were easier for people starting a co-op to get credit.

Cash Flow Projections

More important than the total financial picture is the projection of the cash flow—the amount that is required each month. Just as in buying a house, when monthly payments are often more important than the total price in determining what a person can afford, the monthly cash flow is the most important thing in co-op planning. Money is required at set times to meet mortgage payments, and you must insure that you have the money when it is needed.

There will be points when the cash flow situation will be uncomfortably close. This will occur because individuals may have trouble making payments—some people will be delinquent—and because the financing you arrange may involve lump payments at certain dates. Make sure that you plan the cash flow months in advance so that you know when you will have problems. And when you do, appeal to members to make extra payments or pay off their land entirely to help you over the tight spot. The following article appeared in our paper warning of a problem.

FINANCE COMMITTEE REPORT

The Finance Committee met June 26. Assessing the current cash flow report from M.L.I. (5/9–6/14), the next six months, up until mid-December, look good financially. However, on December 15th we will face a mortgage payment of $22,366, for which we will be $15,738 short.

We presently have $5,974 in the bank. Monthly payments bring in a projected $7,000 on the average. Administrative costs average $645 per month. So adding up the incoming money and subtracting monthly expenses, we project:

8/29	$ 1,684 ahead
9/15	1,789 ahead
11/21	9,999 ahead
12/15	8,104 ahead
12/15	15,738 behind

The Finance Committee looked over the payouts by M.L.I. over the past months, and these cash disbursements to individuals selling their land totaled $11,140.61. The Finance Committee decided to present its report to the Council for further discussions.

Co-op members came to the rescue, so the co-op was in no danger of not meeting payments. Some wrote letters pledging to make extra payments, others paid off their land early, some contributed to the co-op loan fund, and still others got outside loans to pay off their land. None of these things cost the members anything. Those who got bank loans to pay off their land ended up paying interest to the bank on their loans, instead of to the co-op, and in some instances they were able to get a lower rate of interest.

Building Your Net Worth

As mortgages are paid off, and as the value of land increases, the co-op's net worth will increase. In figuring net worth you subtract liabilities from assets. Assets include money in the bank and the value of land; whereas liabilities include mortgages payable, and loans made to the co-op. Within only a few years our net worth rose to over a quarter of a million dollars.

Your co-op may reach a point where it is paper rich but short on cash. After our land was just about paid up, we started to cast envious eyes on the wealth we had built up in equity. Some members wanted the co-op to use this equity by refinancing the land or using the common lands as security for loans. I and others had serious moral qualms about using the land in this way because people had not agreed to this before we purchased our land. It seemed wrong to have people paying on their land, thinking they would own it outright, and then remortgage it. It would be a good idea if people made decisions on whether to eventually use the equity that is built up before you purchase land.

Getting Deeds

People can get deeds before the co-op's total acreage is paid for. Percentages of the land can be released from mortgages, as those percentages of the mortgages are paid up. One year after our co-operative was formed almost one half of the members had paid off their land, and their land was released. The co-operative issued deeds to these people, which gave them clear title to their land.

Many of the legal functions of the co-op, such as issuing deeds, don't require a lawyer. You might want to hire a lawyer at the initial stages to help you purchase land and to teach you how to issue deeds, etc. Make sure that you get a lawyer who will be willing to show you how to do things. We are fortunate to have two barristers in our community, but we still hire an outside lawyer occasionally. Most of the routine legal work, such as issuing deeds, we do with volunteer labor.

Mistakes & Surprises—
Or Where Did the Development Money Go?

Our original projection called for over $100,000 in development money. Now we think we will be lucky if there is $40,000 for development. Where did the development money go? It got dribbled away in lots of little things, such as the co-ordinator's salary, legal fees, and money that should have come from a separate assessments account.

As mentioned earlier, there should be a separate assessments account to cover day-to-day expenses. Development funds should be used for large scale improvements rather than maintenance. There is a difference between building a road and maintaining one. If you do not separate the funds for maintenance, you will find yourself with no development funds.

It is a bit of a mystery for us to figure out where our development funds went. I think that several thousand dollars were lost because of our early policy of buying back people's land when they left the co-op. We returned people's equity and interest payments in some cases, which means that the co-op gave money to the bank that individuals should have given. We also lost money when we financed new land purchases at the old rates. People buying in late were offered the same terms as those who had bought in early. This also added to our accounting expenses because those who bought in late were given ten years to pay for their land, which kept us in the financing business that much longer. I would advise that once the land in a co-op is sold, the co-op remove itself from the business of financing land and let individuals arrange their own financing.

CHAPTER
· THIRTEEN ·

PREPARING FOR CONSTRUCTION

Y our community has signed for the purchase of land. You and all the other members are making payments despite the fact that you don't even know what particular acre will be yours. You're in for at least a month of frantic activity before anyone can settle on the land.

Surveying the Land

First, you must plan your land and have a plat recorded at the courthouse along with your purchase agreements and mortgages. After drawing a map, which is all the plat really is, you will have to get the land surveyed and then divide it among yourselves.

In planning the land, you will want to have many different studies done including a topographical map, an ecological map, aerial maps, and water level surveys to see what areas are flood prone. You might also want to have an engineer check your plans for roads; we regretted that we did not do this as we watch our roads wash away when we have a heavy rain.

Finding the water line—the level of water after the heaviest rain—is necessary so you don't sell someone land that is too wet for a house. Septic tanks cannot be placed in wet land. In conducting a survey to find the water line, you first try to determine the highest point water reaches when it rains and then identify all points on the land below that level. You might find the high water mark by examining the land after a large rain storm during your main rainy season. People from your land-search committee may remember the water level during the rainy season. Still another way of telling the high water line is to examine the vegetation for plants that survive best when partially submerged for part of the year. Once you have one point as a reference, you will be able to mark all areas below that point by using a transit.

A transit is a tool that can accurately line up angles on the land horizontally, like a protractor, and can also indicate lines parallel with any point vertical to the land. You might think of the transit in the latter case as a long level; it even has bubbles in it. Like a level it works on the principle that an air bubble will stay trapped in the middle of the liquid only if the liquid is parallel to the earth. Once you find the high water mark, you can use the transit to find all points parallel to that one and then, by sighting, how much they extend above or below the reference point.

Surveys are really too important to be left to amateurs. We did our surveying ourselves and regretted it later. A couple of acres designated as private home sites turned out to be too low for that purpose, and the co-op had to refund money on those acres. In addition to the water line survey, we also did boundary surveys, and once again we made mistakes. Our mistakes were so bad that some homes were built on the wrong land, and people had to reshuffle boundaries or buy extra acres to maintain ownership of their houses. When people went for bank loans, the bank refused them because title companies wouldn't insure the titles without a professional survey. Loans were granted only after new surveys were conducted. I would strongly advise starting out the right way with professional surveys.

Planning the Land

The actual plan of your land will depend in part on its lay and the water level, in part on your desires. In regard to desirable plans, you might want to consider several factors.

First, you might want to consider placing a community square or park in the center of activity. A commons area provides a place to meet. It might be desirable to have a swimming area and eventually a community center in this park. Many cities have been built around commons, such as the St. Stephen's Green in Dublin, the Bois in Paris, the Plaza in Cuernavaca, or the Commons in Boston. Old cities were traditionally built around a large commons areas with plans not much different from the plan of the Northwest Kingdom, an extension of the M.L.C.

Another factor to consider is the use of common lands as a buffer between private acres. So that many people may border common land, it's better if the common land takes a jagged shape with

112

fingers extending between people's land. If there is something special on the land that everyone will want to enjoy, such as a river, a sinkhole, or a lake, you might want enough common land to insure that everyone has access. In accord with your desire to live with nature, you will want to let the natural features of the land determine your plan for it.

In planning the shape of individual home sites and roads, it is better to have curves and odd shapes than straight lines and rectangles. Curves and odd shapes will give you a greater feeling of privacy. You can't see very far on a curved road, and people won't be as likely to speed, which will cut down on both the wear of your roads and the chance of accidents. If everyone had a square acre and built in the middle of it, you would have much less privacy than you have with odd-shaped acres and people building according to the features of their land.

I have a very large acre of land. You probably thought that every acre is the same size. Acres don't seem the same size. Mine is larger than most because it is triangular, and I border the road only for six feet. A square acre that bordered a road on two sides would lose 250 × 10 × 2 feet. I have a 150 foot walk from the road to my house; you can't even see my house from the road. I built in the extreme corner of my land to be away from my neighbor and so I can look out on common land, which includes an overgrown lake. The lay of my acre is just what I wanted and what I argued for when we were formulating our plat.

Dividing the Land

The process of formulating a plat and dividing the land might be conducted simultaneously. There are several things you can do to aid both processes. We had a questionnaire which tried to identify the types of land each person desired. A committee studied the individual preferences and made tentative assignments of land. Then we had a land party, with a committee assigned to help people find their land. That done, people reacted, negotiated, and the borders were changed on the basis of feedback.

Our co-operative went way out of its way to try to please everyone. At one point an individual decided that he wanted an acre across the road from his original acre. After buying that acre he complained there there was a road in the middle of his land. So to accommodate him we moved the road. Then he sold his land for personal reasons. Now we are left with a strange U turn in our road, which is quite appropriately named Long and Winding Road.

One would think that there would be many disagreements over the assignment of land. We tend to think that everyone will want the same acre that we want. That is not so. People have different interests. Some people wanted all open land for gardening; others wanted all climax forest. Those who wanted two acres were looking at different pieces than my one acre lot, and those who wanted six acres were looking at still other places. Many people had joined the co-op in groups of friends and were more interested in being next to their friends than in getting a particular acre. A few wanted to be on a county road so they could qualify for FHA financing, while others wanted to be as far from the county roads as possible.

Roads

You're going to need a tractor to clear roads and, if you decide on dirt roads, to maintain them. A used tractor costs about $6,000. In addition to use on the roads, a tractor with a back hoe attachment can be used for clearing brush on people's land. Using a tractor for clearing land makes good sense. I spent about a hundred hours trying to clear sumac from my acre before paying a local farmer $20 to do it. He did in an hour more than I had done in a hundred hours.

The first step in creating roads is to survey where they are to go and mark the location with flags. Because the easements for roads are thirty feet wide while the actual roads are nine feet wide, you have considerable leeway, which allows you to go around some trees. Many trees still will have to be cut and their stumps removed, which calls for a party.

We have had dozens of work parties on our roads. They are a pleasant occasion to get together. Men, women, children—all can take part. The co-op provides beer and lemonade. The agenda consists of digging around the roots of trees and then pulling the stumps out with the co-op tractor. Labor is volunteer, with people feeling no compulsion to work any harder than they want to. Sometimes people talk more than they work, but somehow the work gets done.

Once the official roads are mapped, it's important that people use the official roads and not the roads that existed before you bought the land. The more the new roads are driven on, the more they will look like roads. The old roads may go through the middle of a person's property and using them will confuse everyone about the boundaries.

114

You might name the roads and put up signs. I suggest that you take the naming of roads seriously. I think that everyone was in an odd mood when they named our roads. We have names like "Sisow-tobell Lane," "Tan Mouse Road," and "Lois Lane Lane." How would you like to have to put "Long and Winding Road" on your letters? That's the street I live on.

There are several options on how to put in roads if you have the money—and only one if you don't. Dirt roads are dirt cheap to put in, but very expensive in time and materials to maintain. We started with dirt roads and found that they weren't adequate in a few areas where the rain washed the road away. Where dirt roads didn't hold, we used soil cement, which looks just like a dirt road but holds up much better.

If you have the money, I'd advise you to fix a road right when you have trouble. You don't want the kind of trouble that residents of Tan Mouse Road had. As described in our newspaper:

> Tan Mouse residents have been dealing with the grim realities of limited access and egress for four and a half years. We've brought in tons and tons of sand, clay, clayey sand, limerock, stone, brick, gravel, asphalt, concrete, steel and even aluminum runway tracks to fight the monster called Tan Mouse Road. We've stuck dozens of vehicles of all shapes, drives, and sizes for up to a week at a time. We've spent countless people hours working on the beast (and continue to do so), only to acknowledge that we are still at its mercy.

Tan Mouse Road was finally fixed by using soil cement. It works fine and looks like a dirt road. We put the money into Tan Mouse Road because it was our worst, and we keep repairing the other roads. The road I'm on is one of the worst. As my four and a half year old neighbor, Orenda, says, "The name of the road should be changed from Long and Winding Road to Long and Winding and Bumpy Road."

Electricity

As mentioned before in the discussion on covenants and ease-ments, it is possible to negotiate with electric companies over the placement of electric poles. We did negotiate with our rural electric co-operative after some individuals had had experiences with the destruction of trees. Our representatives expressed the view that pre-serving the natural environment, particularly the trees, was our main interest. The electric company expressed the view that their main concern was that they had to have fifteen foot easements to avoid legal suits. The company suggested that we form a three person committee to handle individual problems. Each time the company put in wires they first marked off the path the wires would take and the trees they thought they'd have to cut. Then individuals whose land was affected could examine the path and speak to the committee. The signature of members of this committee were necessary to grant the electric company an easement, so the company made every attempt to protect our trees.

Water

Having pure water would be reason enough to want to live in a land co-operative. People in my land co-op drink water from underground springs. The total cost to me of having this wonderful water pumped right to my house was less than $500 and has cost me less than a dollar a month for the past five years.

We decided on what is called the cluster method of providing water, which for us meant having up to eight households on a well. We chose the number eight because there were county ordinances which mandated treating water if the group were larger. The cluster method was thought desirable over its two main alternatives—having the electric co-operative put in a large water system and having individuals put in their own wells. A large water system was undesirable because, in addition to having to drink treated water, we would not be able to control who was put on the water system, and thus we would lose control of our own water supply. The individual route was thought to be too expensive and a bit of a waste.

Our co-operative of 100 households was divided into 18 clusters, and people were given some option to change clusters. It happened that wells of different sizes could be put in according to whether you had four, six, or eight households, and our clusters varied in size accordingly. Since we were buying 18 wells we were able to bargain on installation price and to buy parts such as well casings in bulk.

Our method of financing the wells was to charge each household an equal share of that cluster's expenses for drilling, installing a pump, and running pipes to all the houses. Those who could afford to do so were encouraged to loan money to any members who did not have the funds. In cases where it was necessary, the co-operative loaned money to clusters to insure that persons who needed water, but were located in a cluster where other persons were unable to cover well costs, would not be forced to install individual wells.

116

My cluster had a 200 foot well installed and then ran the pipes to our houses by ourselves. It is amazingly easy to do. Using a tractor-like machine called a "ditch witch," you simply drive over the area you want to lay the pipe. The machine digs a three foot ditch. Digging took one full day. Next you lay the pipe alongside the ditch, either PVC pipe or copper. Copper is prohibitively expensive, so we used PVC, even though we have some reservations about it as a petro-chemical. PVC is easy to work with. You just swab a chemical on the ends and hold them together until they dry. Our entire water system for eight households took four people two days to install. We had 2 inch PVC running to each area that serves two or more homes, 1½ inch pipe going toward each home, and ¾ inch pipe connecting the system to a house. In all we laid 1,000 feet of 2 inch pipe and 550 feet of 1½ inch pipe. My next door neighbor and I also installed an irrigation system so that we have spigots in our gardens. We always have plenty of water pressure.

CHAPTER
·FOURTEEN·

COMMUNITY PROJECTS

A nother thing that has brought our community together, in addition to celebrations, is community projects. We've banded together to provide activities for our children and also to combat fires, politicians, and mosquitoes.

Providing Activities for Children

Any community that's any good takes care of its kids. People with kids and people without kids, young and old, care about the kids in our community. Many people volunteer to provide activities such as the ones listed below, and we are all concerned when there are problems.

PLANS FOR SUMMER FUN
The following "Schedule of Events" is the result of a group of folks who have been meeting to plan some summer activities for children of all ages. Each Friday night a detailed plan for the following week will be gotten together, so everyone should feel free to offer an activity or share talent and time at a week's notice. Activities are planned for June 25–August 24 . . . Typical days of the week look like this:

MONDAYS *are pretty loose. They are a great day for field trips, skating, horseback riding, kite making, bagel baking . . .*

TUESDAYS *are a day for participation in the summer program at the Community School. Activities are offered through the Parks and Recreation Department; co-oper Patience is on the staff. She will take anyone (adults are encouraged to come too) at 8:00 a.m. on Tuesdays and Thursdays if they meet at the mailbox.*

WEDNESDAYS *are an arts & crafts morning which will be alternated with trips to the library with Agnes.*

THURSDAYS *are days for participation in the recreation program at the Community School.*

FRIDAYS *are busy days. Lisa has offered to take kids swimming in the late morn/early afternoon. We'll alternate between lakes and pools. More adults are needed to go along. Evenings (7:00–9:00) are a family nite featuring song, dance, new games, films. All are welcome!*

Children in our community have much more contact with adults than children in a normal community. Children are welcomed by all into the community. When they are little they are held by all at our meetings. As they grow they can play freely, secure from automobile traffic. People share child care, supervised by co-op parents and not disinterested professionals. We have our own preschool activities and run a program of activities during the summer. Children have their own "town council" and are welcome to attend and participate in the regular one. When community problems arise, children are encouraged to participate in their solution.

One member of the co-op, Gerry, has noted that "persons in the land have made reference to neighborhoods, cluster groups, etc., being akin to family." Long a student of family life and child development, Gerry believes we are doing something very healthy. He quoted several authors in our community paper whom he believes share that view. I include these quotes here.

"We must change our national way of life so that children are no longer isolated from the rest of society. We call upon all our institutions— public and private—to initiate and expand programs that will bring adults back into the lives of children and children back into the lives of adults. This means reinvolvement of children of all ages with parents and other adults in common activities and responsibilities." (White House Conference on Children, Forum 15, 1970)

"Children who had grown up in cluster groups would have a very different view of what they may become from the view we are able to have today. Americans have overvalued personal autonomy and independence. Bringing up children within the isolated nuclear family, we can do little else. Growing up instead with cluster groups, children would experience new forms of interdependence and responsiveness so much needed in the modern world." (Margaret Mead)

Fighting Fires

A friend of mine once expressed the view that the very model of an activity that is good is fighting a fire. Whereas waging war is the

120

model of destructive behavior, fighting fire is the model of an activity that combats destruction. Everyone has an interest in having the ability to fight fires, and we are all thankful to the individuals who organized our volunteer fire department.

Today we have a beautiful bright yellow firetruck parked on our land and over twenty co-op members trained as firefighters. We protect the entire area around our land co-operative. The creation of our volunteer fire department has not only provided us with fire protection; it has also earned us the respect and friendship of our neighbors.

There are many different jobs that have to be done to start and maintain a fire department. Not everyone has to ride in the truck and wear a red hat—though that's half the thrill for many. A fire department has to have an organization with a secretary so it can apply for funding, and it requires a treasurer and bookkeeper to keep track of donations. And of course you have to have many people who are willing to knock on doors to get the all important financial backing of the community.

We were very fortunate to have a retired gentleman in our co-operative who was willing to be our fire chief. He visited every house in our area to get our department started. We were also fortunate to have an individual who was experienced at writing grants who filled out the forms which culminated in our obtaining a surplus fire truck. After the initial stages of organization, a publicity campaign was conducted and benefit concerts held.

In addition to fund-raising and applying for grants, a lot of energy will also go into training firefighters. A certified Red Cross instructor conducted classes on our land, and people from the local forest rangers' station showed us a movie and—by burning brush on our common land—demonstrated techniques for fighting brush fires. For further training, those who are part of our regular department truck force have attended firefighters school.

Our fire department had no sooner formed than it was fighting a fire on our land. One of our members was burning trash in a barrel when the fire spread to about 1,000 square feet of dry brush around her house. The community responded. A half dozen people used firefighters' sprayers, and a chain was formed to keep them full of water. We didn't have the truck yet, but were able to put the fire out with rakes, hoses, and sprayers.

Many people, including the fire chief in the nearest city, have been impressed with the co-op volunteer fire department. He didn't expect the department to last, because most volunteer departments don't last, but the enthusiasm of the co-op volunteers has impressed him. A newspaper article attributes the success of the volunteers to the fact that co-op members are accustomed to volunteering their time and working together.

The department is going strong. Recently it got a second truck, members are now connected with radio communications, and a fire station is in the works. The dedication of these firefighters is remarkable. At a fund-raiser for the department attended by representatives from the Division of Forestry, other fire departments, and the county politicians, the Chief's Award was given to sixteen year old James, who made it to thirty-seven of the fifty fires the volunteers had responded to so far that year. When James missed the truck one time, he pedaled his bicycle two and a half miles to catch up. That's devotion.

Controlling Politicians

When there is a threat to our land, individuals do not have to face the threat alone. There is strength in numbers, and with that strength it is possible for each individual to protect his land. A solitary individual can have his land ruined when a dump is put next to his land; a community can put up so much resistance that the dump has to be relocated.

Our first indication that we were threatened with a dump next to our land came when a member spoke with a county commissioner and learned that there was to be a public meeting to consider placing a dump next to us. Engineers had already been boring holes and found the soil and rock content satisfactory for a dump.

Our community went into action. There was a flood of letters and petitions. Every meeting of the county commissioners was filled with over a hundred of us. People were spilling out into the halls. It got so that county meetings were an occasion for us to see each other. It was like old home week. We also worked with larger groups such as a neighborhood association that collected money for legal fees. Our people put flyers in mailboxes throughout the area to insure excellent attendance at any meetings that were held. The net result was that the county found another place to put the landfill.

Almost everyone in our community, except for one recalcitrant anarchist, votes. On election days a stream of cars leaves from our community mailbox. People list when they are leaving to vote in case anyone wants a ride. At the polls it is old home week—the same way it looks when the county commission is considering anything that we're concerned about.

The last time we voted we elected two of our members as the local precinct captains. Perhaps we should work more closely with our neighbors and form a slate with others so that not everyone who is elected in this area is from our land co-operative. It must be a bit bewildering for the people who've lived around here all their lives to suddenly find that outsiders have a majority of the votes. No devisive issues have arisen yet. We enjoy the good will of the community for our work in forming a volunteer fire department, fighting the placing of a dump, and the good things our people are doing with the local school. Still, we must be careful not to flex our political muscle too strongly when we can achieve the same goals by working with our neighbors.

When someone runs for local office in our community—for school board or for county commissioner—they are certain to come out to get our support. They know that we all vote and that we have a tendency to discuss issues together and then throw all our votes for one candidate, and they want those votes. Several times we have scheduled "meet the candidates" affairs at our community center. Every candidate is invited to attend to face our questions and solicit our support.

Our success has been mixed so far. We have helped to elect one commissioner whom we like and are working on school board, county, and congressional campaigns. Our energy is not regular, and the loose coalition that elected the county commissioner has not been strengthened to the point where it can put forward other candidates. The pieces for a strong coalition exist in our community, just as the pieces exist in other communities in the United States. We have yet to put it together. Once we do, we will start running candidates for all offices in our area and we will win.

Controlling Mosquitoes

We haven't been as successful at controlling mosquitoes as we were in controlling our local politicians in preventing a dump. Many articles have appeared in our newspaper discussing the mosquitoes, but like the weather, no one has done anything about them. Actually I don't think we have much of a problem, but that could be because they don't find me attractive. One approach would be to kill the mosquitoes; another would be to control what you eat, so they won't eat you.

To get an idea of what our mosquitoes are like you might want to read this report on an actual occurrence reported by Katie.

KIDDO. . . . MOSSKIDDO!!

Pa and I were asleep in our tent the other night, camping next to our vegetable garden at the Misty Hills Land Co-op, when two voices outside our door startled us awake. They said that they were hungry, and could they please have something to eat? Well, it sounded kind of strange to me, but I began to scrounge for apples and cheese while Pa unzipped the tent flap about half way.

I heard Pa yell and zip the tent flap up real quick, but not before I turned and caught sight of two BIG mosquitoes. Pa dove for the Cutter's lotion, and we gooped it on. We know you are not supposed to goop it on, but those were BIG mosquitoes. Anyway, we guessed we would find out just how well that stuff works.

By this time the mosquitoes about had the tent flap unzipped. Thinking fast Pa said, "I hear that if you carry a cross in front of you, a mosquito won't touch you. Is that right?"

"Depends on how fast you carry it, mister," the first mosquito drawled. He was in the tent now. He grabbed the end of my sleeping bag and was trying to dump me out of it when I heard him say to the other mosquito, "Hey, shall we eat them here or take them back to the woods?"

"Are you kidding? You know as well as I do that if we take them back to the woods, those BIG mosquitoes will take them away from us!"

For several months one article after another appeared on how to combat the mosquito problem, but then interest died when we started thinking that the cure might be worse than the problem. This article by Tom appeared on the conducting of a mosquito survey:

NOTES FROM MOSQUITO SURVEY HEADQUARTERS

The Theory is that if we know who is biting us, we'll know how to stop it. So then the task is to capture some of the enemy to learn of their species and their relative numbers (relative to the total population of mosquitoes).

Brave volunteers are at this minute shedding their blood to learn these secrets. Herman, Billy, Tom, Laurie and Norine, Chuck, Mary, and Glenn are collecting the enemy. But it is not enough!

We need killing jars (old spice bottles will do), a source of chloroform or carbon tetrachloride (300 ml of ether), and we need more collecting stations here on the land. Think before you leap to the fore and give me a hand because it's not really a lot of fun and it must be done on a regular basis.

Twice a day, a day and night sample is taken by each station. For 15 minutes the collector places a tender, blood rich piece of meat—arms and legs are the usual—on the altar of mosquito survey.

Then when the little devil lands for a fill-up, the killing bottle is placed over it and it basks in chlorinated hydrocarbons for a few seconds and then discorporates.

At the end of the collecting time, the suckers who have fallen for the trap are divided into groups according to species, and their respective numbers are noted. Some as yet undisclosed persons will identify the corpses. There are ways of dealing with these creatures, once they are identified.

People either ran out of blood or patience because no results from the survey were ever tabulated. Instead articles appeared discussing an insect growth regulating hormone called Altosid SR-10 that works as a larvacide rather than a pesticide. Altosid SR-10 has been approved by EPA and is thought to be effective in doses of only 3 to 4 ounces per acre, with only 0.3 to 0.4 ounces of active ingredient. The cost was also thought to be desirable at only $1.50 to $2 an acre.

We felt secure that we would soon have a means to combat mosquitoes. Using a compound that is chemically similar to the juvenile hormone present in mosquito larvae would certainly do the trick and would have other advantages over pesticides, including its low toxicity to higher organisms, effectiveness with small dosages, and its tendency to be biodegradable within ten days. The disadvantages were that we were not sure if other larvae would be affected and wanted more testing done of this compound. Our attitude was to wait with the knowledge that relief was on the way.

Meanwhile people had suggestions for how to keep from being bitten. It's common knowledge that some individuals are not bothered very much by mosquitoes. So that you can be one of those lucky people, you might be interested in the substances you can eat that will keep mosquitoes away. One substance that will keep them off is B-1 (thiamine), another a sulfur substance called Allicin, found in garlic, which is supposed to increase the body's ability to absorb vitamin B-1. So if you eat lots of garlic and B-1 rich foods like brewer's yeast, the skeets will leave you alone. Members made testimonials to this mixture.

My brother Ben ate brewer's yeast and garlic like it was mullet and grits. We were on the beach one night, and when we got back Mary counted about 50 bites on my back alone, but Ben wasn't touched. I wouldn't have believed it myself if I hadn't personally and painfully witnessed it.

He stood there, still, arms out-stretched, in the nude, baying at

*the moon; and I was jumping, slapping and hopping, and they passed
him up and ate me.*

We've tended toward individual approaches to the mosquito
problem and shied away from changing the environment. I don't
have much of a problem around my home and would like the environment left alone. Sometimes I can count a dozen dragon flies while
sitting outside, and I'd hate to hurt these mosquito hawks. Maybe
someday we'll make a collective war on mosquitoes as we started to
do. Our love of the land and desire to keep things natural has the
upper hand now.

A WHAT YOU CAN CHIEVE

PART FIVE

CHAPTER
• FIFTEEN •

LIVING YOUR DREAMS

Most people dream of achieving financial independence. People in our community have no illusions that they will be able to do everything within each household; they only hope that all the members of the community together can be independent of jobs outside the community. Our land co-operative tries to help members gain financial independence.

Financial Independence is a Community Affair

Any large group of people, and certainly a group with one hundred households, has a tremendous economic potential. As discussed in the introduction, a hundred households, each having a yearly income of $10,000, collectively have a million dollars a year coming into their community. Most communities don't do much with these resources because the money also goes out of their community.

There is an analysis that compares the money flowing out of a community with the situation of colonialism. Consider the situation of an imperialist country and its colony, the situation that the Thirteen Colonies once had with respect to England. Under colonialism any money that is made in a colonial area must be spent in the imperialist country, insuring that the wealth remains centralized in the hands of the imperialists. Many economists believe that the black ghettos of America are comparable to colonies, and I might add that the analysis works for suburbs also. People make money in jobs but spend it at the large shopping centers instead of in their communities, so that the resources end up in the hands of the few corporations that own the large chain stores. More and more of the wealth ends up in the hands of a few people.

The ideal situation for a community is to have money coming in from outside and to spend most of that money in the community. In this way the residents of the community gain wealth. Two things aid in this goal. One is to have businesses that keep your money in the community, and the second is to have businesses that bring outside money into your community. The entire community has an interest in promoting enterprises of both sorts.

Most of the people in our community joined the land co-operative in the hope of being able to drop out in style. Land co-operatives are not just another form of residential development. While at the first stage we function as a consumer co-operative in the purchase of land, our concerns for providing alternative lifestyles for our members go beyond the consumer co-op model.

To some the concern we have for alternative means of earning a living is an outgrowth of our development as a community. Economic enterprise is one more way we deepen our relationship together. Burt expressed this view in our paper.

> A community is like a vine, a living growing entity.
>
> We have arrived at that point: the vine can continue to grow along the ground and share those things that it can share with the ground; the vine can climb a tree, engulfing it and growing with it.
>
> The vine on the ground is in a safe position, enjoying the sun and taking its nourishment from mother earth through its deepening roots.
>
> The vine that grows with the tree relies on its roots to nourish the entire vine, while the vine ascends toward the sun.
>
> The ground vine will eventually be trampled or cleared away, for such is the fate of ground clinging vines.
>
> Vines that ascend but do not choke the tree develop a stronger root system, put out healthier leaves, and become as a tree itself, still growing long after the ground has been cleared.
>
> We, as a community, need a tree if we are to remain a community. We must recognize this need: an attracting force that will allow us to continue to grow and keep us cohesive. The difference between us and any other subdevelopment is that sense of community, of family. Since this community is of prime interest to my family, I wish to fertilize the vine and the tree.
>
> I believe that the tree can take the form of a community enterprise.
>
> I feel strongly that we should develop an economic interest by and for us. As the vine, we can grow with and around this interest and become stronger for it. Without it, we chance our roots being too shallow and lose all if the wind starts blowing our soil away.
>
> This is my view.

To further our economic goals we formed a financial planning committee. As stated in our paper,

The goal of the Financial Planning Committee is to create a financial base within the community, to generate work and revenue for co-op employees. We feel that an economic bond will be critical to continued cohesion as a community. We intend to generate excess revenue from this base to be used initially to establish diversity and long range stability for the business(es) managed by the committee. This accomplished, these monies shall be at the disposal of the co-operative.

We feel that to achieve these goals we need to have the authority and responsibility to make management decisions within the committee. This we seek from the owners of the business(es), that is from M.L.C., with guarantees of accessibility to all records and meetings for co-op members and a pledge of professionalism in management tempered with humanistic co-operative goals.

It is our intention to search within and beyond our community, seeking experience and sound advice with regard to all management decisions. We are aware that an enterprise can only occur with support and approval by the membership at large and accept all of the limitations set forth in the covenants and restrictions.

As this statement of policy is ratified, the financial boundaries prescribed by the membership will be set forth, and the committee will make a solicitation for applications to the development program. We intend to help all applicants meet guidelines set forth by the committee, for the benefit of the co-operative. The committee would also like to use some monies for basic economic research such as zoning and licensing requirements, so we will also propose a quarterly budget based on the scope of development indicated by the membership.

Our Financial Planning Committee is a self-appointed open group of co-op members. To appoint yourself, please attend three consecutive announced meetings.

Any time co-op members can buy something from another member of the community, rather than giving money to one of the chain stores, wealth is kept within the community. A good place to begin is with the most immediate needs of the community members— housing and food. A community of a hundred families has tremendous resources which are spent on both of these needs.

As soon as the co-op is organized and people start building homes, tremendous resources are made available for people to earn a living building homes. Before joining the co-op people had been spending at least one-fourth of their income on housing. Figuring an average income of $10,000, this means that people have a quarter of a million a year to spend on housing. Actually there are much greater resources because each household could borrow $20,000 from a bank for homes which would generate over two million dollars. With two million dollars you could theoretically hire everyone in the community to work at constructing homes for a year, since labor costs are approximately half the cost of construction.

Community Based Businesses

Construction Companies

A large constrrction company which is based in our community got its start building homes in our land co-operative. Some members of this company actually got loans for the homes which they built, which means that they borrowed money to hire themselves to build their own homes. After the company got started it moved on to doing homes throughout the area, and more recently it started a solar home development adjacent to the land co-operative. The total amount of building done by the company during the last year was in excess of a million dollars, which makes it one of the largest in our area. Sixteen of the thirty-four members of the company and all its officers but one are members of our land co-operative.

This company, Mad Dog Design and Construction, has been doing pioneer work in creating energy efficient homes. Their methods include the use of earth piled against outer walls, called berm construction, the use of extra exterior walls, called envelope construction, the use of barrels filled with water to retain heat, and most commonly, the use of glass on a southern exposure. Their houses work—they save energy. In fact Mad Dog is so confident of their houses that they have introduced the Guaranteed Maximum Energy Bill. They guarantee in writing that a family of two buying a house in their latest development will pay no more than an average of $50 a month ($600 a year) for total electric and gas usage. The figure is $60 a month for a family of three. Their guarantee is truly a revolutionary concept in home construction.

There are several other construction companies owned by community members. Accuracy Ltd., Inc., recently converted a house in town to apartments. Neil Ryder Construction and Design, Inc., is currently developing two new subdivisions in addition to building houses. Live Oak Concepts, Inc., has done home remodeling and recently built a convenience store in a unique style that uses post and beam construction. They call their style "cowboy modern."

134

Independent Carpenters and Cabinet Makers

There are many individuals who enjoy construction work but don't like to work with a large company. Several such persons are able to earn a living in our community doing work on their own schedule. I hired a couple of my neighbors to work on building my house. The final trim work was done by a co-op member who does fine cabinet work. These individuals worked when they wanted and kept track of their time. My neighbors who work in this manner report that they usually have all the work they desire.

Contractors for Painting and Landscaping

David Tolley is a painting contractor. His company did a fine job spraying a special solar reflection paint on the roof of my house. I buy all my plants from a neighbor who has a company called "Growing Concepts, Inc." They do natural landscaping and outdoor woodwork, including decks, porches, and fences. This company has provided occasional work for up to six people.

Brown Bag Lunches

Along with shelter, food is a basic necessity that can support someone. During the transitional phase, and to some extent after, individuals will be working in town, and those individuals will have to eat lunch. One enterprising co-op member started a business making brown bag lunches. On my way to work in the morning I pick up my lunch in our community mailbox and pay $2 a day for this service. The lunches are the best organic fare and well worth the money; besides, I'm happy to help a fellow community member gain financial independence. By making twenty lunches a day, which takes two hours every morning, this co-op member is able to earn a hundred dollars a week, which she finds quite adequate for living in style on the co-op.

A Bakery

There are many part-time businesses that people can start which can potentially become full time. Several people get together on Sundays to bake bread. The bakery is not primarily a money-making operation. People get much more than just money from baking bread together. As Nancy described it in our paper:

> *Bread baking brings us close to simplicity—it connects our thoughts and movements with nature's blessings to us. With each kneading of the dough, we realize the wonder of our environment and our interaction with our surroundings—we feel the connection of*

135

nature's resources, and our ability to respectfully appreciate these resources and life's unfolding brings us into unity with a source of goodness and love for life. I like the saying, "Love is not only the most important ingredient: it is the only ingredient which really matters."

Food Co-op and General Store

People in our community are also active in co-ops throughout the area; in fact members of our community have worked as the co-ordinators of the largest food co-op and general store. A couple of individuals are able to support themselves by working for these co-ops, and many members of our community gain discounts on food and supplies in return for working at the co-op stores. These co-ops also provide an outlet for us to sell produce and products from our home cottage industries. Members have sold pottery and wooden tool boxes in the co-operative general store.

An Alternative School for Children

The Grass Roots Free School is based on the teachings of A. S. Neill expressed in his book *Summerhill*. The school teaches children to function in a democratic society by practicing democracy. All rules, except those related to health and safety, are made on a democratic basis with children and adults having one vote each, and the rules apply to everyone equally. After being a member of our land co-op for many years, the school's founder, along with six other co-op members, started another land co-operative to serve as the home of their school. They purchased forty-five acres, four of which are for the school. The school, which serves thirty-five children, is staffed by seven part-time employees and volunteers.

Specialty Shops

Several shops in town are owned by co-op members. The Unicorn Shop specializes in natural fiber clothing, dancewear, toys, flowers, and gifts. Food Glorious Food sells both fresh and frozen dinners and lunches. People can eat in or take out. Their specialty is fresh wholesome food with no preservatives. Those who want fresh food without cooking can pick up any number of dinners or have Food Glorious Food provide catering services. A third store is the Morning Glory Shoppe, which sells womanmade clothing and gifts.

The Morning Glory Shoppe is a project of the Morning Glory Collective, a woman owned business. This business started when four women in our community and three from the alternative community at large got together to sew. They made enough from selling clothing and embroidered shirts at local craft shows to start other endeavors. In addition to the shop, the Morning Glory Collective is trying to organize women crafters and markets woman-recorded albums, womanmade quilts, and a product of their own called an Everywoman's Calendar. Their beautifully illustrated calendar allows a woman to record her body rhythms. Those using it say it gives them a better sense of self-awareness. You can get more information on the calendar by writing to the Morning Glory Collective at P.O. Box 1631 in Tallahassee, Florida 32302.

Another product developed by a member of our community is the Birthing Doll. The Birthing Doll is a twenty-two inch silkscreened ragdoll that delivers a baby by regular delivery or Caesarean. A child can pull the baby out to see where we come from, and even detach the "umbilical cord." This doll has been mentioned on the Johnny Carson Show and on wire services by the UPI and Associated Press. It has also been mentioned on the B.B.C. and on television in France and Italy. Information on the Birthing Doll is available from Monkey Business, Box 20001, Tallahassee, Florida 32304.

Artists and Craftspeople

There are many artists and craftspeople on the land. Joanne Chamberlain crafted a custom stained glass window to fill a skylight over our bed. She has also done stained glass work on windows made by Bullard and Ball, Inc., a company owned by two co-op members, that produces the finest handmade furniture, windows, doors, and entryways in our city. Joanne's husband, Paul Chamberlain, is an artist who works at hand blown glass. Other artists include Janet Falciglia, a custom jeweler who works in silver and gold, Leslie Reimer who does freelance calligraphy, Chip Bloyd who is a leathersmith, and Bob Celander, Dee Dee Shand, Rick Rice, and Glenn Sharron who are graphic artists. Bob Hill has a music studio out here, and David Hastings is a poet who lives in our community. The number of creative endeavors by people in this small community of one hundred households is too numerous to list them all.

Agriculture

Small Scale Farming

Individuals have been able to supplement their incomes by selling fresh produce from their home gardens. Sometimes produce is sold immediately to neighbors. As I drive home on Long and Winding Road in the co-op, I check a sign my neighbor puts up advertising what he's selling. Whenever I need what he has, I stop because I know that his produce is organic and his prices are reasonable.

Some people report that one problem with buying produce from neighbors is that people have a hard time just buying produce without chatting for hours on end. When they arrive home with their vegetables, they find that it's much later than they'd like: their day is shot. Unconsciously, and often consciously, the time spent is thought of as a cost of getting the vegetables, so people tend to just buy in town. The lesson of this is that it is desirable to have a market either on or off the land with set times for buying and selling.

It didn't take long for one of my neighbors to sell his crop. Tom has a set offer from his next door neighbor for all the corn he can grow. The family that buys the corn has a freezer, so they can enjoy fresh corn all year round. They freeze the corn immediately after picking to preserve the vitamins.

Large Scale Farming

We haven't really tried full scale farming—our land isn't really appropriate for it. We don't have a large spread of twenty acres or so that we can farm with our tractor. Most of our common land is wet, with just enough dry land for a community center and small park. It would be good for a co-op to plan on having a large area for farming as a communal enterprise.

In growing salad vegetables or grains you have handicaps compared to the big farmers who dominate the market. Most food is grown on huge conglomerates that have the advantages of using machines at every stage. A land co-op enterprise is labor intensive rather than capital intensive. In growing most crops this difference results in making it impossible for a co-op to undersell the big producers. You would get a share of the market only if people were willing to pay more for organically grown vegetables. None of the factors that would hurt your chances of selling vegetables apply to orchards, which are labor intensive.

Honey

Several co-op members keep beehives and enjoy a harvest of fresh honey. To start out you plant trees that will nourish your bees. We have been planting tupelo trees for several years and, as noted in our paper, they are taking root.

IF TUPELO TREES ARE HERE, CAN THE BEES BE FAR BEHIND?

That's the thought that was in our minds when we saw the new growth on the tupelo trees. It might be a while before the trees have enough blooms to support many bees, but the seedlings which Diann and David provided for us are taking hold and looking strong. Having never seen a tupelo tree, we're anxious to see what the full-blown model looks like. We planted some near the lake and some up on the hillside to see which location is the best, even though we understand that they grow best in wet areas. (Some people just can't be told.) If you planted some tupelo trees, check them out and enjoy; if you didn't, come by and help us enjoy ours.

A Nonprofit Research Institute

Several of us on the land started a nonprofit institute, the Alternate Futures Institute. The institute received a $14,000 grant its first year and was able to provide some income to two community members. As stated in its bylaws:

The purposes of the institute are to promote awareness of trends and issues relating to the future of our community and beyond, to stimulate thought and discussion on alternate futures, and to conduct research and education on behalf of humanity and the survival of life on the planet. Areas of research include, among other areas, ecologically derived sources of energy, agriculture, aquaculture, and housing that is consistent with sound ecological practice.

Our hope for the institute is to establish a research park to demonstrate the potentials of solar energy and organic agriculture. The emphasis would be on technologies that are already known to work, such as hot water heating and passive solar construction. Small scale buildings utilizing passive solar principles would be constructed, and school children and interested adults would be guided through the demonstration buildings. There might also be a farming project to educate the public on the principles of organic agriculture. Careful scientific experiments would be conducted, and the experimental farm would be open to the public at set hours.

Our community is not really appropriate for housing the institute we started. There is no tract of land on which we would want to have the influx of visitors that the institute would require in order to succeed in its mission of educating the public. Most of us value our privacy and don't want large numbers of visitors. Another land co-op might be started that centers on the AFI or a similar institute.

Members of such a co-op could support themselves with research, educational programs, and grants.

Some Personal Dreams

Everyone has their own special dreams of what they would like to do with their lives. Somehow our dreams don't seem to fit existing jobs. There are many people who would like to do things that would benefit society; but instead they end up working at jobs that don't use their talents. In a land co-operative you can share dreams and hopefully bring them to fruition. I'll share some of my personal dreams with you.

Wellington Press

With the publication of this book, Wellington Press is no longer just a dream. In addition to this book, I have written four others that I hope to publish. The next book to be released, *How To Work For Peace,* is what I call a peace polemic. In it I argue that peace should be defined as the nonviolent settling of international disputes and that peace requires an international authority, and I list many positive steps that might be taken for peace. Should my books sell, I would like to have Wellington Press become a regular publishing company. There are many talented people in my community who could do the editing and graphics work that turns manuscripts into books.

Land Co-op Consultants

A natural business for people in a land co-op is starting other co-ops. Recently, the M.L.C. bought thirty-nine adjacent acres, developed it as part of our co-op, and realized a profit. That profit made possible the construction of a beautiful community center that both old and new members now enjoy.

It's my hope that people reading this book will want to start their own communities. There isn't room in my community for more people—our land sold out years ago—and we're not equipped for visitors. My hope is that the idea will spread, and people will form new land co-ops. I don't want my community to get any larger, and I certainly don't want hordes of people descending on us. As I wrote in our paper when we were considering buying a tract of land across the street from us:

> *Suppose we succeed in doubling the size of the co-op? We'll end up with a huge organization that can no longer be run on a personal*

140

and informal basis. When someone puts a note on the mailbox about a party there will be twice as many people. When you go to co-op functions, you'll see a lot of strange faces because we'll be a big crowd. I, for one, find it hard to relate to large numbers of people at once. There is an optimum size for a community. Small is beautiful.

I would, however, like to see kindred communities spring up near our co-operative. While I don't want the Misty Hills Land Co-op to grow larger, I'd like to see other co-ops around us to protect the environment. In addition I believe that there are different things that are possible with additional numbers of people in the area. With several communities of people we might have more businesses, have a market, and do some large scale farming. Our political strength would grow, which would enable us to protect this area before it is ruined by developers.

I think that the land co-op I describe here is a desirable place to live and would like to help advise people on how to form their own communities. So that there could be a follow up to the publishing of this book, my wife, Judy, and I incorporated a company called Co-operative Enterprises, Inc., and decided to call a division of it Land Co-op Consultants. I describe what it might do at the end of this book. In thinking of how people might support themselves while starting co-ops, it appeared to us that the most sensible thing would be to get licenses to sell real estate. In real estate, sales commissions are customarily paid by the seller, and most people sell their land through brokers. Judy and I are getting our licenses and are going to try to keep up on available land so that we can help people who are interested in starting land co-ops. Any group using our services would have a committee that checks out all available land and comparative prices to insure that they get the best price possible.

Peace Travel, Peace Game

Another activity of Judy's and mine has been the invention of a peace game that we hope to market and the planning of what we call "Peace Travel." In my book on how to work for peace I advocate conducting conferences attended by citizens of both the U.S. and the U.S.S.R. at which participants brainstorm on ways of working for peace. We hope to organize international travel packages for those who would like to travel and work for peace.

Survival University

The last dream I'll share is my desire to be part of what I call a "survival university." I'm a philosophy professor who is obsessed with

141

the problems that relate to survival on this planet, and my survival university would combine my interests and background. I shared my fantasy with my neighbors in our paper.

A FIT OF FANTASIES by Dave Felder

SURVIVAL UNIVERSITY MOVES TO NEW HOME

   S. U. has just completed the move to its new home bordering the land co-op. The curriculum includes courses related to both personal survival and the survival of humanity. As part of studying for personal survival, students learn to build houses, farm, and to fix machines. The curriculum on global survival includes courses in ecology, history, economics and most of the usual academic disciplines; only at Survival University everything is applied to survival issues. As part of the curriculum students spend several months as traveling organizers, during which time they sharpen their speaking and writing skills.

The issue of world survival takes us beyond one little community to a discussion of how to have an impact on the world outside our community.

CHAPTER
• SIXTEEN •

IT'S MORE THAN AN INVESTMENT

So far I've shown you how, by purchasing land in a loving community, you can apply money that is now going for rent or mortgage toward owning your home outright, how you can get ahead of the game and even invest, and how you can end up working for yourself. I think I've shown you that buying land in a loving community is a good investment. It is in fact the best investment you might make. But buying land in a loving community is much more than an investment.

Making The World Better

After our basic needs have been taken care of, after we have our homes paid for and enjoy financial security, most of us humans want to do something to improve this world of ours. We hear the news and realize that humanity, and indeed all other life on this planet, is threatened with destruction. I think that most of us would like to help change this situation. Living in a loving community can help you become active in making a difference because you can draw on the energy of others.

Historically, many social theorists, including Karl Marx, have criticized the view that one can change the larger society by forming an intentional community. I believe that the criticisms given in the past of utopian attempts do not apply today. This is apparent when we consider why the utopian societies did not have much of an impact in the past.

Utopian Communities: Past and Present

Previous communities did not change society because the outside system was able to go along as it had been doing. Those who went off simply dropped out of the mainstream, and their passage had no effect on the rest of society. Oh, it is true that many creative ideas can be traced to communities like Oneida, but such communities had no effect on the body politic. People were able to drop out, and they did so. Society was able to continue as before, and it did so. And the one had no effect on the other.

There are many factors today which nullify the traditional criticisms of alternative communities. First the mainstream society is in trouble; it cannot continue as before. Our alternative communities are providing alternatives not just for the members of these communities. They are providing alternatives for everyone in the areas of energy and fighting inflation with a simpler lifestyle.

A second factor that is different today is that we cannot drop out of mankind's problems no matter how much we may want to. When the Shakers formed their communities, they did not have to worry about nuclear bombs or ecological disasters. Today our lives are threatened no matter where we live on this planet. People in our community are more aware of these dangers than most people. We work actively to promote change that will lessen the threats to life on our planet.

A third factor that is different is that we are not simply dropping out of society; we are building a society of our own. The approach of a land co-operative differs from the individual approach to dropping out in that we are forging a new community with new institutions that support our community. We do not pretend to be able to do without people but instead are forming complex networks with support groups all around us.

Unlike the groups of the sixties which united people only in the area of ideology, we are uniting people together in their very livelihoods. Ours is not a unity of one aspect of our existence but a unity in every aspect. People in the movements of the sixties had to sell themselves on the labor market and take the trappings that went with their establishment jobs. We are providing people with new alternatives. There are now many people who have dropped out of the establishment.

Marx criticized the Utopians for believing that they could change people by just changing their ideas. He believed, like Feuerbach before him, that man is what he eats. As Engels stated at Marx's funeral oration, Marx discovered that man must first of all eat and produce before he can think. The error of the sixties was that people's minds were won over, but they still had to sell their bodies. Those who bought those bodies claimed those minds. Today we are listening to the admonition that people must first of all eat, and we are making it possible for people to eat without selling themselves.

We are forming the core of a new society within the womb of the old. I say the core because not everyone who will work for change will come from alternative communities; but many of the leaders will. The leaders will be made up of the elements that are free of the control of the established forces, just as the leadership of the civil rights movement came from the only institutions not controlled by whites—the black churches. The alternative communities will perform a role which is analogous.

We are living the ideas others only talk about. Members of our community are pioneers in the Appropriate Technology that E. F. Schumacher preached. We have deschooled our society, as Ivan Il-lych urges—members of our community design houses and run business without the dubious benefits of diplomas. We are redoing economics by strengthening the household economy and helping to unravel the centralized system of exploitation as we get free of it. We may not be rich, but we are no longer among the poor who are rendered helpless to improve their own condition. As soon as we bought land in our community, we gave ourselves the power to improve our own lives and the power to effect change in the larger society.

There are several ways that a community such as the land co-op I describe helps a person to become a change agent. One way is by providing an alternative model for how a society might be. A second way is by being a center for political activity. I describe each of these.

Providing An Alternative

Intentional communities provide an alternative which can help humanity to survive. Using an evolutionary model, the more variations there are within a species, the greater the chance the species has of surviving. What if the mainstream society starts to fail? Suppose that gasoline becomes too expensive to keep the trucks going that feed people in the cities. Suppose petroleum based fertilizers become too expensive to use. What are people going to do? They will certainly want to look at a community that is self-sufficient and uses organic gardening in their search for answers.

I believe that it will benefit the larger society greatly to study the alternative communities that are based on a simple lifestyle alternative. Many people in our community believe that our community has something to offer society, and we want to contribute toward solving the contemporary problems of energy, food, and the search for peace.

The simple lifestyle alternative is one that is often mentioned but little understood. E. F. Schumacher, Hazel Henderson, and Governor Jerry Brown, among others, speak of the need for Americans to simplify their lives and consume less. While many speak of the need for a simple lifestyle alternative, few have changed their own lives or know what the simple lifestyle is. Similarly, those who criticize the simple lifestyle alternative, such as Herman Kahn and President Ronald Reagan, have no idea of what this alternative is.

Two researchers who have studied the co-op, Lynn K. Harvey and Thomas M. Harrington, concluded that the co-op represents an alternative value system. In their study (available through Land Co-op Consultants) they asked, "Does involvement in the M.L.C. represent an attempt by 'typical Americans' to secure one aspect of the 'American Dream'—home ownership—or does the co-op provide a living arrangement which is part of a lifestyle that expresses an alternative value orientation?" Their research paper contrasted two value systems, one based on materialism and one based on environmental concerns. Two issues that divide the viewpoints are whether one accepts an occupational or a personal definition of success and whether one accepts increased or decreased consumption as a goal to work toward. Their conclusion, after interviewing co-op members, is that the co-op is much more than another development—it represents an alternative value system.

One element of the alternative value system is a value on underconsumption which is opposed to the prevailing conspicuous consumption. Below is a section of their report.

> Another goal that seemed common to the sample of interviewees was that of reducing material consumption and spending. The basis of this goal seemed to stem from several origins. One was a concern for the environment and a recognition of the damage done to it by a heavily industrialized economic base. These people saw the necessity to reduce their material standard of living as a step in the direction of reducing the environmental strain caused by manufacturing.
>
> The respondents who were either retired or facing retirement within a few years saw the need to adapt to a reduced standard of living gradually, so that they could learn how to cope with a smaller

income and the effects of inflation on a retirement pension. One woman said:

> My motive (for moving here) wasn't entirely philosophical, you know. I'm approaching retirement age, and I wanted to step down my expenses and way of living. I had been renting houses in town. I have five children, and I moved out here when the last one was in high school. It was easy to see the day when I wouldn't need such a large house.

Others saw reducing their material consumption as a means of avoiding the eight to five urban work routine while providing time to pursue activities they felt to be of more value. One man said:

> Neither of us is looking to work 40 hours a week for the rest of our lives, but then again we're not looking to make a fortune, either. We feel we're putting it into proper perspective. What we're saying is we'll be satisfied to get along on less than an average income because of the way we handle our money. And because we choose to do things that don't require a lot of money, we have more freedom to do other things we want to do.

Just by living in a land co-op a person is contributing toward change because intentional communities are experimental communities. The environment is one that encourages innovation.

Helping to Preserve Scarce Resources

Just by our reducing our own consumption, we are helping to preserve scarce resources. With only five percent of the world's people, the United States consumes more than thirty percent of the world's resources. This cannot continue. The people of the world, who are fighting to increase their standard of living, will not allow it to happen. They will make the materials we have been getting from them increasingly expensive. We will either have to go to war with the world, or we'll have to learn to live more simply. We must live simply so others can simply live.

Many people are looking for *the* solution to the energy problem. They view the energy problem as one of finding a replacement for oil. Oil is now burned in utility plants, oil runs our transportation system, and oil is running out. It would seem that the problem is finding something to take the place of oil, but this is wrong.

I say that the energy problem appears to be one of finding a replacement for oil because our real need is to have a way to heat water, run refrigerators, heat homes, and power cars. Oil has been a unique fuel in the history of energy because it has great diversity—it can both heat homes and power automobiles. Before oil, one energy source—horse power—was used for transportation, and others were used for heating homes.

People speak of finding *the* solution to the energy problem. There may not be one solution, but instead many partial solutions—one for each of the functions oil now serves. People in the land co-op are finding ways to save oil. Our solutions should not be criticized for being partial. It is entirely possible that a patchwork of partial solutions will fulfill our energy needs.

Being a Center for Change

I believe that alternative communities and institutions will perform an important role in the formation of a new political force. There are those who write of consciousness raising and believe that changing people's minds by itself will bring about change. I believe that consciousness raising is an important element but that political organization is essential. Let me explain how that organization might come about and how alternative institutions might be important to the process. In order to present my grassroots theory of change, I would like to begin with an analogy.

The analogy, which will help explain how a new political force might emerge, is from Dr. Herbert A. Simon's book, *The Sciences of the Artificial.* Dr. Simon considers two watchmakers, Tempus and Hora. One of the watchmakers builds watches from all individual parts, and the other uses intermediary units. To quote Dr. Simon:[1]

> The watches the men made consisted of about 1,000 parts each. Tempus had so constructed his that if he had one partly assembled and had to put it down—to answer the phone, say—it immediately fell to pieces and had to be reassembled from the elements. . . .
>
> The watches that Hora made were no less complex than those of Tempus. But he had designed them so that he could put together subassemblies of about ten elements each. Ten of these subassemblies, again, could be put together into a larger subassembly; and a system of ten of the latter subassemblies constituted the whole watch. Hence, when Hora had to put down a partly assembled watch in order to answer the phone, he lost only a small part of his work, and he assembled his watches in only a fraction of the manhours it took Tempus.

---

[1] Herbert A. Simon, *Sciences of the Artificial* (Cambridge, Massachusetts: M.I.T. Press, 1969) p. 91.

The analogy is, of course, to the seeking of national power by isolated individuals versus the building of alternative institutions as an intermediary step. Land co-ops, food co-ops, environmental groups, and political action committees could all come together to form a new national political force. And if an attempt to form a national political party fails, these subassemblies will still be in place to try again.

Intentional communities, food co-ops, and other people's organizations might fit together into a new political coalition. But what type of coalition might it be? How large should it be, and what should it espouse?

I would like to see a coalition for world peace, and that means it should be international. Previous movements for peace have been national and have been aimed at criticizing the nearest national government. I'd like to see a movement that is international and stresses what all people have in common. The best way to get people together is to have them face a common enemy. That enemy is all the dangers to human survival. The political party I envision might be called "The International Survival Party," ISP for short. It's purpose would be to awaken people to the dangers threatening human survival, so that people would come together in peace to solve their problems.

Is this visionary? Is this crazy? Here I am living in the woods, in the middle of nowhere, calling for the founding of an international party. I'm getting used to doing the impossible. It's easy when you can find a dozen close neighbors who are willing to listen to you. Intentional communities provide an atmosphere where things become possible. I never did any construction work, but I ended up building a house. I never had any money, but now I have investments. Now I've written a book, so I'm an author. My neighbors are doing the work of contractors, architects, farmers, and executives, all without being certified. We are turning dreams into reality. We are creating an environment in which all things are possible.

THE APPENDIX

APPENDIX • ONE •

MODEL SET OF COVENANTS AND RESTRICTIONS

In this model set of covenants and restrictions I include no restrictions on either the sale or rental of properties. The covenants and restrictions of the Misty Hills Land Co-op includes extremely detailed rules covering both the sale and rental of properties. Some of these were included to insure that adjacent landowners would have first priority in the purchase of land. Experience shows that most people will be sensible enough to offer their adjacent neighbors a first chance to buy their land, and when this is not done, there is usually a very good reason, such as an individual selling an acre to a best friend. In the latter case and in many other cases, people have ignored the restrictions of the Misty Hills Land Co-op regulating the sale of properties. Rather than have unworkable restrictions, I recommend a set of covenants which has no restrictions on either selling or renting property. Of course, it is up to each group to decide what rules they want to live by. These are only suggestions.

Article I—*Definitions*—This article defines the words used in the rest of the documents such as "members," "common lands," etc.

Section 1. *Definitions.* The following words when used in this Declaration of Covenants and Restrictions or any supplemental declaration of covenants and restrictions have the following meanings:

(a) "Land" means all such existing property and additions thereto as are subject to this Declaration or any supplemental declaration according to the description and provisions of Article II.

(b) "Common land" means those areas of land, whether or not shown on any recorded subdivision plat filed by the Cooperative, intended to be devoted to the common use and enjoyment of the members.

(c) "Dwelling" means the building or structure in which one family unit resides, whether or not said family unit is comprised of persons related by consanguinity.

154

(d) "MLI" means the Misty Hills Land, Inc.

(e) "Cooperative" means the Misty Hills Land Cooperative.

(f) "Owner" means any sole or part owner of land in the Misty Hills Land Cooperative.

(g) "Purchasing unit" means the owner or majority of the part owners of any parcel of land in the Cooperative.

(h) "Member" means a person who is an owner of land in the Cooperative.

(i) "Resident" means a person who has continuously resided in the Cooperative for 60 days.

Article II—*Property subject to this declaration*—This article has the legal description of the land.

Article III—*Environmental Protection*—This article stated that we have natural preserve areas in which 80% of the land must be left in its natural state, and it lists specific restrictions on the removal of trees.

Section 1. *Natural preserve areas.* The Cooperative shall establish certain natural preserve areas in which all clearing, cutting of trees, and other alterations of the natural vegetation shall be limited as described herein: No more than 20% of the contiguous area or part thereof of each acre in a natural preserve area shall be cleared or cut. In such areas, 80% of all land area in each acre must be left in its natural state except for brambles, poisonous plants, dense vines, and other use-inhibiting vegetation, as defined by the Governing Board of the Cooperative. In the event that an owner owns more than one acre, only 5% of each additional acre may be cleared as described above, in addition to 20% of the initial acre, except for minimal roadways where obviously necessary to provide access. Notice of intent to clear shall be given in a manner convenient to all members if such clearing will result in plants or trees that could be moved and utilized by other owners.

Section 2. *Restrictions on removal of trees.* Trees on any part of the land shall be protected as set forth herein: No tree over 12 inches in diameter shall be removed from any land which is subject to these Covenants and Restrictions unless one or more of the following conditions are present:

(a) Necessity to remove trees which pose a safety hazard to pedestrian or vehicle traffic or threaten to cause disruption of community services;

(b) Necessity to remove trees which pose a safety hazard to buildings;

(c) Necessity to remove diseased trees or trees weakened by age, storm, fire or other injury;

(d) Necessity to observe good forestry practices, i.e. the number of healthy trees that a given parcel of land will support;

(e) Necessity to remove trees in order to construct proposed improvements as a result of:
   1. Need for access around the proposed structure for construction equipment.
   2. Need for access to the building site for construction equipment.
   3. Essential grade changes.
   4. Surface water drainage and utility installations.
   5. Location of the proposed structure so as to avoid unreasonable economic hardship.

(f) Necessity to remove trees for garden space if open land is inaccessible, so long as the percentage limitations contained in Section 1 are not exceeded.

Section 3. *Definitions.* "Tree" means any woody plant having at least one well-defined stem of at least 3 inches in diameter measured at a height of 4.5 feet above the natural grade. "Removal of a tree" means any act which causes a tree to die within a period of two years, including, but not limited to: damage inflicted upon the root system by machinery, storage of materials, and soil compaction; changing the natural grade above the root system or around the trunk; damage inflicted on the tree permitting infection or pest infestation; excessive pruning, paving with concrete, asphalt or other impervious material within such proximity as to be harmful to the tree.

Section 4. *Penalties.* Violations of these provisions are subject to liquidated damages of up to $100 for each one inch of diameter of all trees removed and up to twenty cents per square foot of prohibited clearing. All fines shall be finally determined by the Governing Board and these fines may be revalued every five years to reflect any upward change in the consumer price index.

Section 5. *Enforcement.* The above sections relating to environmental protection shall be enforced with or without legal action by the Governing Board of the Cooperative. The Governing Board shall be the exclusive judge of the nature of all violations.

Article IV—*Density*—This article states that the minimum parcel of land which shall be owned, held, or occupied is one acre and that no more than six adults, eighteen years of age or older, shall reside on any one acre of land.

Section 1. *Parcels.* No parcel of land shall be owned, held, or occupied which is less than one acre in size, except that small parcels may be owned, held or occupied in areas designated by the Cooperative as business areas for commercial ventures. No parcel of land shall be owned, held or occupied which is more than 10 acres in size unless approval is granted by the Governing Board of the Cooperative. This provision shall not apply to the Cooperative.

Section 2. *Residents.* (A) No more than six adults, 18 years of age or older, shall reside on any one acre of land, and in no event shall more than twelve persons reside on any one acre of land. However, exceptions for good cause may be made by the Governing Board. (B) If a parcel contains more than one acre, density shall be determined by the average number of persons per acre in such parcel.

Section 3. *Dwellings.* No dwelling shall be constructed or maintained on any parcel of land which is less than one acre in size, and no more than one dwelling per acre shall be constructed or maintained on any parcel of land. This restriction may be waived by the Governing Board.

Article V—*Architectural Control*—This article is aimed at promoting the harmonious integration of buildings with the natural environment, the creation of energy efficient homes, and compliance with building and sewage system requirements. The article also allows the use of mobile homes and camping facilities for the convenience of individuals building homes but rules out the presence of mobile homes and campers after a stated date.

Section 1. *Residences.* The Governing Body of the Cooperative shall assist households in planning the location and design of residences on the land in order to promote the following:

(a) The harmonious integration of buildings with the natural environment;

(b) The creation of energy efficient homes; and

(c) Compliance with safe construction techniques and sanitary waste disposal practices.

Section 2. *Mobile homes.* No mobile homes, or modular homes which may be used as mobile homes or permanently attached to the land, as defined and identified by the Governing Board, shall be allowed on any residential lot after September 1, 1978. However, the Governing Board may allow variances from this restriction based on economic necessity for periods not to exceed one year at a time.

Section 3. *Camping.* Nothing in these restrictions shall prohibit members from camping on their land or from utilizing a camping vehicle or abode for such purpose for a period of one year. After one year of continuous use of the camping facility as a residence, no camping will be allowed unless approval is obtained from the Governing Board.

Section 4. *Excavations.* No excavations of any type shall be made without the prior approval of the Governing Board.

Article VI—*Prohibited Activities*—This article rules out hunting, lethal weapons, dangerous and destructive animals, offensive outdoor lights, loud and/or dangerous vehicles.

Section 1. *General provisions.* No noxious or offensive activity shall be carried on upon any part of the land. Nothing shall be done on the land which may be or become an annoyance or nuisance to the neighborhood. The provisions of this Article shall not be construed to prohibit farming activity.

Section 2. *Animals.* No dangerous or destructive animals shall be allowed on the land. The Governing Board of the Cooperative shall supervise control of any offensive activity of animals.

Section 3. *Hunting.* No hunting shall be allowed on any part of the land, except for protection from a poisonous or dangerous creature. "Hunting" means pursuing any animal with intent to harass, tease, disturb, wound, maim or kill.

Section 4. *Weapons.* No use or display of guns or other lethal weapons shall be allowed on the land, except for self protection as allowed by law.

Section 5. *Vehicles.* No noxiously loud or dangerous vehicles shall be operated on the land. No motor shall be used on any boat for any purpose on any lake, pond or stream located on the land.

Section 6. *Lights, signs.* No offensive outdoor lights or illuminated signs shall be permitted on the land.

Section 7. *Violations.* The Governing Board shall be the exclusive judge of the nature of all violations.

Article VII—*Ingress and Egress*—Article seven gives to the governing board the right to grant road easements and the right to regulate traffic on the land.

Section 1. *Road easements; conveyance to county.* Members of the public and all residents living on the land shall be allowed to travel over those easements recorded in the Leon County Public Record after September 1, 1973. Each owner or part owner agrees to convey such portion of said easements at such time as Leon County should decide to accept title to such roadway easements, and the membership by ⅔ vote should decide to have such title so conveyed.

Section 2. *Regulation of traffic.* All traffic on such easements shall be subject to the reasonable regulation of the Governing Board of the Cooperative.

Section 3. *Access routes.* Temporary or permanent access routes which would connect parcels on the perimeter of the land to public roads are specifically prohibited, unless authorized by the Governing Board in writing.

Article VIII—*Easements*—This article gives to the governing board of the co-operative the right to grant easements over, under, and through any of the property subject to the declaration for the purpose of operating and maintaining electrical, water, or sewer lines. This article is absolutely essential to get electrical companies to run wires to households.

Section 1. *Authority.* The Governing Board of the Cooperative is hereby empowered and authorized to grant easements over, under and through any of the property subject to this Declaration as described in Article II, for the purpose of constructing, operating, maintaining, and/or removing any electric, water and/or sewer lines and related facilities as well as pedestrian paths or other common uses of the land. The Governing Board is further empowered to grant easements which are necessary for similar uses not specifically described herein.

Section 2. *Restrictions.* No herbicides may be used on any easements on the land, and all easements shall revert to the servient estate if the easement is not used for any of the permissible uses for a period 30 years. Easements on land designated as natural preserve shall not be subject to the restrictions set forth in Article V, Section 1.

Section 3. *Enforcement.* No easement shall be valid or enforceable unless the Governing Board notifies all owners of property over, under or through which the easement would run, at least 30 days prior to the effective date of the easement. If any owner disagrees with said easement, no action shall be taken until the matter is put to a vote of the membership. The decision of the membership shall be final.

Article IX—*Commercial Ventures*—This article states the type of businesses that will be allowed and where they will be allowed.

Section 1. *Commercial areas; approval of Governing Board.* The Cooperative shall establish certain areas located on the common land in which the operation of commercial business ventures for profit shall be allowed. However, no such commercial venture shall be allowed unless approval is granted by the Governing Board of the Cooperative according to the criteria and procedure established by the Governing Board.

Section 2. *Assessments.* The Governing Board shall assess the owners and operators of commercial business ventures in such amounts as are necessary for the maintenance of commonly owned properties and facilities in the business area and for other appropriate purposes.

Article X—*Common Land*—This article states that every member of the co-operative shall have the right and easement of enjoyment in all of the common land.

158

Section 1. *Right of Enjoyment.* Every member of the Cooperative shall have a right and easement of enjoyment in all of the common land, and such easement shall be appurtenant to and shall pass with the title to every purchasing unit.

Section 2. *Use as collateral.* Use of the common land by the Cooperative as collateral for financing improvements and development of the land shall have prior approval of at least ⅔ of all members.

Section 3. *Improvements.* Buildings and improvements of a permanent nature made on common land and any activities that alter the nature of the common land shall have prior approval of the Governing Board of the Cooperative.

Section 4. *Business areas.* Common land in the business area shall be sold or leased as determined by the Governing Board.

Article XI—*Assessments*—This article grants the right to the co-op of making assessments for the purpose of improvement and maintenance of properties, services, and facilities devoted to, or related to, the use and enjoyment of the community.

Section 1. *Method and purpose of assessments.* Annual and/or special assessments shall be levied by a majority vote of all members of the Cooperative and administered by the Governing Board for the purpose of promoting the health, safety, and welfare of the residents of the community and, in particular, for the improvement and maintenance of properties, services, and facilities devoted to or related to the use and enjoyment of the community.

Section 2. *Common land taxes.* Assessments shall be levied in amounts sufficient to assure payment of common land taxes.

Section 3. *Creation of the lien and personal obligation of assessments.* Each owner of a parcel hereby convenants by acceptance of a deed or contract for deed, whether or not so expressed therein, to pay to the Cooperative annual or special assessments as provided in Section 1. These assessments shall be fixed, established, and collected from time to time as established by the membership. No lien or personal obligation shall arise from a special assessment unless the Cooperative can certify that the owner of each parcel so assessed has had adequate notice of the assessment. The assessments, together with interest and costs of collection, shall be a charge on the land and shall be a continuing lien on the property against which each assessment is made. Each assessment, together with interest and cost of collection, shall also be the personal obligation of the person who was the owner of the property at the time when the assessment fell due.

Section 4. *Priority of liens.* All liens provided for in this or any Article contained in this Declaration of Covenants and Restrictions shall be absolutely subordinate to the lien of any first mortgage placed upon the property subject to these Covenants and Restrictions before December 25, 1975.

Article XII—*Membership and Voting Rights*—This article defines voting members.

Section 1. *Voting Rights.* Members who own land may vote on all issues. Residents and children of members may vote at the discretion of the land owners they live with.

Section 2. *Limitations.* The number of voting members permitted to vote on any issue presented to the membership of the Cooperative shall be limited to six votes per acre represented.

Article XIII—*Governing Board of the Co-operative*—The composition of the governing board and the process of its selection are specified in this article.

Section 1. *Governing Board; officers.* The voting members of the Cooperative shall select a Governing Board consisting of seven members. The quorum necessary to all valid action of the Board shall be not less than five. The Board shall establish such offices and officers as they deem necessary for the proper management of the Cooperative and shall conduct its activities in accordance with the Constitution.

Section 2. *Powers and duties.* The Governing Board shall have the responsibility and authority to make decisions involving protection of the environment, development of common properties and facilities, the planning of economic enterprises and common activities, the arbitration of disputes involving members, the collection and disbursement of funds, and in all other matters necessary and proper to the management of the Cooperative.

Section 3. *Sovereignty of the membership.* A majority of the voting members of the Cooperative shall overrule the Governing Board on any decision. A member of the Governing Board may be recalled and removed from office by a vote of ⅔ of the members. Votes shall be taken either at a meeting assembled or in writing.

Article XIV—*Enforcement*—This article states how long the rules (C&R) shall be in effect (fifty years) and how they are enforced—by the governing body, by community arbitration, and by legal enforcement if necessary.

Section 1. *Covenants and Restrictions binding; term.* The Covenants and Restrictions of this Declaration shall run with and bind the land, and shall inure to the benefit of and be enforceable by MLI or the Cooperative or their respective legal heirs, successors and assigns, for a period of 50 years from the date of this Declaration, after which time said Covenants and Restrictions shall be automatically extended for periods of 80 years in the event any single owner shall request extension.

Section 2. *Community arbitration.* In any dispute between members, an arbitration committee may be appointed by the Governing Board of the Cooperative to investigate the problem and to report its findings to the Governing Board. The Board shall then make a decision, binding upon the members involved, which will resolve the problem, or it may empower the arbitration committee to propose a compromise solution with the members involved.

Section 3. *Legal enforcement.* Enforcement of these Covenants and Restrictions shall be by any legal proceeding against any person or persons violating or attempting to violate any covenant or restriction, either to restrain the violation or to recover damages, and against the land to enforce any lien created by these Covenants and Restrictions.

Section 4. *Waiver of minor violations.* Minor violations of these Covenants and Restrictions may be waived by the Governing Board of the Cooperative, which shall be the sole and exclusive judge of the nature of all violations.

Section 5. *Severability.* Invalidation of any of the covenants or restrictions of this Declaration by judgment of court order shall in no wise affect any other provision which shall remain in full force and effect.

Article XV—*Amendments*—This article states that amendments can be made by a vote of 85% of the members.

160

Section 1. *Amendments.* Amendments to these Covenants and Restrictions may be made by an affirmative vote of 85 percent of all members of the Cooperative whose membership can be verified on the date of formal presentation of the amendments to the members.

APPENDIX · TWO ·

LAND CO-OP CONSULTANTS

Land Co-op Consultants hopes to make it easier for individuals who are interested in living in Land Co-operative to join with others in purchasing land. Land Co-op Consultants will try to get such individuals in touch with people who are knowledgeable about land co-ops, developing land, financing, and legalities and will try to provide the following services:

1. Maintain a list of people who are interested in living in land co-ops so that interested people can meet.

2. Send out a newsletter to let people know about co-ops that are being formed.

3. Make presentations on the co-op idea.

4. Maintain a list of individuals who are available to speak on land co-ops and other related topics.

5. Assist in every stage of setting up land co-ops, from providing moderators for initial organizational meetings, through the purchase of land, solving problems of governance, and long range planning.

6. Keep a listing of land for sale that is appropriate for land co-ops. Investigate possible co-op sites.

7. Sometimes arrange for groups to purchase land and sometimes purchase land which is then sold to groups.

8. Provide a complete consulting service for every aspect of setting up and maintaining land co-operatives.

9. Make available to individuals in land co-ops many resources, such as books on home construction and small buildings that people can use while building their homes, etc.

10. Provide life change counseling and financial counseling to individuals who are considering living in land co-ops.

11. Conduct short courses and workshops for people in land co-ops on such topics as passive solar home construction.

12. Serve as a central source of information on land co-ops.

If any of the services listed above interest you, you might want to write to the address listed below.

Land Co-op Consultants
(a division of Co-operative Enterprises, Inc.)
P.O. Box 13504
Tallahassee, Florida 32308

ABOUT THE AUTHOR

David W. Felder is one of the original members of the land co-operative he describes. Having designed and built his own house, he follows the simple lifestyle alternative he examines in this book.

With both a doctorate in philosophy and a master's degree in Instructional Systems, David W. Felder is well qualified to examine both the philosophical implications and organizational aspects of intentional communities. He has been a speaker at new age conferences, peace symposiums, World Future Society meetings, and philosophy conferences, and has published articles in both popular and professional journals on environmental ethics, community, alternative values, energy, international law, and human conflict.

David W. Felder has written four other books including a logic text that he uses at Florida A&M University where he is employed as an Associate Professor in Philosophy, a book on the design of the logic text, a book entitled "Incentivism: An Alternative to Liberalism and Conservatism" and a book entitled "How to Work for Peace." He has received several academic honors including being selected as both a fellow and reviewer of grant proposals by the National Endowment for the Humanities and being selected to participate in the first national workshop on the teaching of philosophy by the American Philosophical Association. When he is not writing, teaching, or traveling, David enjoys gardening, canoeing, and living in his home on the land co-operative with his wife, Judy, and his many warm-hearted neighbors.